Poems from

IRELAND

Poems from

IRELAND

Selected by William Cole
Drawings by William Stobbs

THOMAS Y. CROWELL COMPANY • NEW YORK

POEMS OF THE WORLD

Under the editorship of Lillian Morrison

POEMS FROM FRANCE
Selected by William Jay Smith

POEMS FROM THE GERMAN
Selected by Helen Plotz

POEMS FROM INDIA
Selected by Daisy Aldan

POEMS FROM IRELAND
Selected by William Cole

CONTENTS

INTRODUCTION

In 1853, when Ireland's fortunes were near their lowest, the English poet Walter Savage Landor wrote:

> Ireland never was contented.
> Say you so? You are demented.
> Ireland was contented when
> It could use the sword and pen,
> And when Tara rose so high
> That her turrets split the sky,
> And about her courts were seen
> Liveried angels robed in green,
> Wearing, by St. Patrick's bounty,
> Emeralds big as half a county.

There's some allowable exaggeration there, but the basic truth is that back in the Dark Ages, when the rest of Europe was under a blanket of ignorance, Ireland was dotted with monasteries whose inhabitants were dedicated to learning. By the fourth century A.D. the country was divided into five fairly well-organized clans, under the kingdom of Tara, and the profession of poet was among the most honored. It took from seven to twelve years of specialized study to qualify as a bard. These bards were either attached to a large court, or traveled from court to court as enthusiastically-welcomed itinerants. Their language was Gaelic (or Irish, as I prefer to call it, since a form of "Gaelic" is also spoken in Scotland). Most of the poetry of these bards, and that of the scholars in monasteries, translated today, is not particularly interesting: sagas and eulogies about the exploits and characters of real and mythological chieftains, some religious poetry, and nature poetry, much of the best of which was more or less doodled on the margins of illuminated manuscripts by monks whose attention had strayed from the lettering at hand.

Ireland's troubles with outsiders began in the ninth century with a plague of Norse invaders who only partially succeeded in infiltrating the civilization. In the twelfth century the Normans (from England) invaded and took a claim on Ireland that lasted some eight hundred years. Gradually all rights were taken from the native Irish: their religion was forbidden them (they had been Catholic since the fifth century); they were forced to speak English rather than Irish; they were not allowed to engage in certain professions; they were repressed, oppressed, exploited, and overtaxed. Never a docile people, the Irish frequently rebelled, but were always savagely crushed. There was no education for the native Irish save what they could scrape together themselves. Such a situation is not conducive to poetry, and by the eighteenth century the only poets were semiliterate versifiers and makers of street ballads.

The great potato famine of the eighteen forties almost saw the death of the race: a million Irish died of starvation and allied diseases, and another million and a half emigrated, principally to America and Australia. This nineteenth century, which brought so much misery to the country, also saw the beginnings of a new appreciation of Ireland's past. This was in large part due to the work of some Anglo-Irish scholars, notably Sir Samuel Ferguson, who translated myths and poems from the ancient Irish and made them available to the literate public. The Anglo-Irish were, and are, the descendants of the English and Scotch who came to Ireland over the centuries to occupy and rule, to fill the professional roles, and to engage in the more lucrative trades. They were the hated landlords. Almost entirely Protestants, the Anglo-Irish produced a number of great writers whose work fits more into the mainstream of English literature than into any distinct Irish category — Oliver Goldsmith, Jonathan Swift, Richard Brinsley Sheridan — and later, Oscar Wilde and George Bernard Shaw. Some of these old Anglo-Irish families considered themselves as Irish as the native Irish, but this view was never reciprocated. In the nineteenth century there were also some brilliant translations and fake translations done by an eccentric Irish-Catholic, James Clarence Mangan. Coincidental with the work of the scholars and translators, Thomas Moore, the first really internationally known poet of Catholic Ireland, was setting his own lyrics to old Irish harp and folk tunes, which had been uncovered by contemporary musicologists. It is interesting to see that although Moore knew no Irish, some of his "Irish Melodies," as they were called, had a distinctive Irish beat or meter which was obviously influenced by the musical line; his poems introduced rhythms that were entirely new to poetry in the English language — and that were definitely a contribution from the Irish language. For example,

> At the mid hour of night when stars are weeping I fly
> To the lone vale we loved when youth shone warm in thine eye;
> And I think oft, if spirits can steal from the regions of air
> To revisit past scenes of delight, thou wilt come to me there,
> And tell me our love is remembered, even in the sky.

The Irish poet and critic Robert Farren wrote: "One can match that rhythm, and that stanza, many times in Irish, but not in the English of any poet of England." This characteristically Irish "long, wavering line" can be found in many of the poems in this anthology.

The nineteenth-century interest in myth and history led to a poetry of patriotism — not good poetry, but much stirring verse in which the poets, knowing their English oppressors, did not refer directly to Ireland's troubles, but personified their country as a woman — "Kathleen ni Houlihan" or "My Dark Rosaleen."

The eighteen nineties saw the beginning of the phenomenal "Irish Literary Revival," which produced the two greatest writers of their time: James Joyce in prose, and William Butler Yeats in poetry. Joyce left Ireland early and never returned (although Ireland is all he ever wrote about), but Yeats spent most of his life there, and was the pivotal figure around whom revolved a galaxy of poets, playwrights, and all the intellectuals of his time. Among the contemporaries in his long literary life were John Millington Synge, Sean O'Casey, Frank O'Connor, Padraic Colum, Austin Clarke, Oliver St. John Gogarty, Lady Gregory, AE (George William Russell), and James Stephens. Yeats was interested in the myths and sagas of ancient Ireland, and his plays and poems make generous use of them. Although he did not speak or read Irish, he had straightforward translations of the old poetry made for him, and he borrowed generously from them. He wrote: "Can we not build up . . . a national literature which shall be none the less Irish in spirit from being English in language?"

One of the problems in compiling an anthology of Irish poetry is that Yeats tends to dominate it. He was immensely prolific, and was, after all, in the assessment of many critics, the greatest poet of his century. To quote Robert Farren again: "Yeats is Irish. He has tenderness, quietness, pity; rage, love and lust; gaiety, fantasy, indignation; robustness, delicacy, arrogance . . . how many more passions and spiritual weathers? Mockery and reverence surely." It is hard to beat a combination like that, and his prominence tends to dwarf the quite real accomplishments of his fellow poets. Poems of his appear, of course, in every anthology, and they usually are the same poems in each. I have used, in this book, poems that are not so frequently reprinted—with a few exceptions.

The freedom that had been Ireland's dream for eight hundred years began to show signs of becoming a reality after the Easter Rebellion of 1916. In earlier years the poet Padraic Pearse had written a few lines that summed up the history of Ireland. He called his poem "Tara Is Grass":

The world hath conquered, the wind hath scattered like dust
Alexander, Caesar, and all that shared their sway:
Tara is grass, and behold how Troy lieth low —
And even the English, perchance their hour will come!

Pearse, along with two other poets, Thomas MacDonagh and Joseph Mary Plunkett, was executed by the English for his part in the uprising.

Ireland now has her independence from England. She is a nation once again, and is proud, progressive, and on the way to becoming comparatively prosperous. She is still a country of poets; a country where the speech of the poorest peasant has poetry in it; where there is fine poetry in the words of the ballads that are sung in the pubs and in any place where people meet together. Poets are celebrities, and are treated as such. The Irish papers print more — and better — poetry than American or English papers do. Poems are memorized and recited by schoolchildren, and Radio Eireann has regular broadcasts of poetry read by trained verse speakers.

As you will see, the poetry of Ireland is varied; there is poetry of lamentation, poetry of oppression, of the brutality of man and weather, of poverty. But there is also poetry of the joyous side of life: poetry of celebration. The Irish are also music-makers and love-talkers; they extend the invitation, in the words of Yeats's poem, "Come dance with me in Ireland."

I have arranged this book alphabetically by author. This creates some startling contrasts: a translation from the eighth century cheek by jowl with a poem by a young Irishman now in his twenties; an old-fashioned, naive poet alongside a contemporary sophisticate. But I think it creates a good feeling of variety and pace. It also has the advantage, the alphabet being arranged as it is, of leading up to Yeats.

There is a border between northern and southern Ireland, with poets on either side of it. I have ignored this border — would that they could!

WILLIAM COLE

POEMS

WILLIAM ALLINGHAM (1824–1889)

A Dream

I heard the dogs howl in the moonlight night;
I went to the window to see the sight;
All the Dead that ever I knew
Going one by one and two by two.

On they pass'd, and on they pass'd;
Townsfellows all, from first to last;
Born in the moonlight of the lane,
Quench'd in the heavy shadow again.

Schoolmates, marching as when we play'd
At soldiers once—but now more staid;
Those were the strangest sight to me
Who were drown'd, I knew, in the awful sea.

Straight and handsome folk; bent and weak too;
Some that I loved, and gasp'd to speak to;
Some but a day in their churchyard bed;
Some that I had not known were dead.

A long, long crowd—where each seem'd lonely,
Yet of them all there was one, one only,
Raised a head or look'd my way;
She linger'd a moment—she might not stay.

How long since I saw the fair pale face!
Ah! Mother dear! might I only place
My head on thy breast, a moment to rest,
While thy hand on my tearful cheek were prest.

On, on a moving bridge they made
Across the moon-stream from shade to shade,

Young and old, women and men;
Many long forgot, but remember'd then.

And first there came a bitter laughter;
A sound of tears the moment after;
And then a music so lofty and gay,
That every morning, day by day,
I strive to recall it if I may.

ISAAC BICKERSTAFFE (1735–?1812)

Song
(from *Love in a Village*)

There was a jolly miller once,
    Lived on the River Dee;
He worked and sang, from morn to night;
    No lark so blithe as he.
And this the burden of his song,
    Forever used to be, —
"I care for nobody, not I,
If no one cares for me."

An Expostulation

When late I attempted your pity to move,
    What made you so deaf to my prayers?
Perhaps it was right to dissemble your love,
    But — why did you kick me down stairs?

C. J. BOLAND

The Two Travellers

"All over the world," the traveller said,
   "In my peregrinations I've been;
And there's nothing remarkable, living or dead,
   But these eyes of mine have seen —
From the lands of the ape and marmozet,
   To the lands of the Fellaheen."
Said the other, "I'll lay you an even bet
   You were never in Farranalleen."

"I've hunted in woods near Seringapatam,
   And sailed in the polar seas.
I fished for a week in the Gulf of Siam
   And lunched on the Chersonese.
I've lived in the valleys of fair Cashmere,
   Under Himalay's snowy ridge."
Then the other impatiently said, "See here,
   Were you ever at Laffan's Bridge?"

"I've lived in the land where tobacco is grown,
   In the suburbs of Santiago;
And I spent two years in Sierra Leone,
   And one in Del Fuego.
I walked across Panama all in a day,
   Ah me! but the road was rocky."
The other replied, "Will you kindly say,
   Were you ever at Horse-and-Jockey?"

"I've borne my part in a savage fray,
   When I got this wound from a Lascar;
We were bound just then from Mandalay
   For the island of Madagascar.
Ah! the sun never tired of shining there,
   And the trees canaries sang in."
"What of that?" said the other, "sure, I've a pair,
   And there's lots of them over in Drangan."

"I've hunted the tigers in Turkestan,
   In Australia the kangaroos;
And I lived six months as a medicine man
   To a tribe of the Katmandoos.
And I've stood on the scene of Olympic games,
   Where the Grecians showed their paces."
The other asked, "Now tell me James,
   Were you ever at Fethard Races?"

"Don't talk of your hunting in Yucatan,
   Or your fishing off St. Helena;
I'd rather see young fellows hunting the 'wren'
   In the hedges of Tubberaheena.
No doubt the scenes of a Swiss canton
   Have a passable sort of charm,
Give me a sunset on Slievenamon
   From the road at Hackett's farm.

"And I'd rather be strolling along the quay,
   And watching the river flow,
Than growing tea with the cute Chinee,
   Or mining in Mexico.
And I wouldn't care much for Sierra Leone,
   If I hadn't seen Killenaule,
And the man that was never in Mullinahone
   Shouldn't say he had travelled at all."

[NOTE: All the places named by the second traveler are in the County Tipperary.]

EAVAN BOLAND (1945–   )

Requiem for a Personal Friend

A striped philistine with quick
Sight, quiet paws, today —
In gorging on a feathered prey —
Filleted our garden's music.

Such robbery in such a mouthful!
Here rests, shovelled under simple
Vegetables, my good example —
Singing daily, daily faithful.

No conceit and not contrary —
My best colleague, worst of all
Was half-digested, his sweet whistle
Swallowed like a dictionary.

Little victim, song for song—
Who share a trade must share a threat—
So I write to cheat the cat
Who got your body, of my tongue.

EILEEN BRENNAN (1913–   )

One Kingfisher and One Yellow Rose

Taking pity on this scrag-end of the city
Is my one kingfisher
Sitting stiffly on his willow
And staring at my one yellow rose.
I like him for his blueness
And more so for his kindness,
But I wish I had a garden
Then I wouldn't be depending
On this one kingfisher
And on one yellow rose.

There's a man, says one who knows,
Who is always in a hurry—
His mind's on making money
For a garden
Where he harbours
Many a kingly fisher
And many a quality rose.
But he's not the man he was,
Says my one who knows,
Since his fellows stopped saluting him
With: How's your one kingfisher?
And: How's that yellow rose?

J. J. CALLANAN (1795–1829)

The Outlaw of Loch Lene
Translated from the Irish (18th century)

Oh, many a day have I made good ale in the glen.
That came not of stream, or malt, like the brewing of
men;
My bed was the ground; my roof the greenwood above,
And the wealth that I sought—one far kind glance from
my love.

Alas! on the night when the horses I drove from the field,
That I was not near, from terror my angel to shield!
She stretched forth her arms—her mantle she flung to
the wind,
And swam o'er Loch Lene, her outlawed lover to find.

Oh, would that a freezing, sleet-winged tempest did
sweep,
And I and my love were alone far off on the deep!
I'd ask not a ship, or a bark, or pinnace to save—
With her hand round my waist, I'd fear not the wind or
the wave.

'Tis down by the lake where the wild tree fringes its sides,
The maid of my heart, the fair one of heaven resides:
I think, as at eve she wanders its mazes along,
The birds go to sleep by the sweet wild twist of her song.

J. J. CALLANAN

The Convict of Clonmel

How hard is my fortune,
  And vain my repining!
The strong rope of fate
  For this young neck is twining!
My strength is departed,
  My cheeks sunk and sallow,
While I languish in chains
  In the jail of Clonmala.

No boy of the village
  Was ever yet milder;
I'd play with a child
  And my sport would be wilder;
I'd dance without tiring
  From morning till even,
And the goal-ball I'd strike
  To the lightning of heaven.

At my bed-foot decaying,
  My hurl-bat is lying;
Through the boys of the village
  My goal-ball is flying;
My horse 'mong the neighbors
  Neglected may fallow,
While I pine in my chains
  In the jail of Clonmala.

Next Sunday the patron
  At home will be keeping,
And the young active hurlers
  The field will be sweeping;
With the dance of fair maidens
  The evening they'll hallow,
While this heart once so gay
  Shall be cold in Clonmala.

[NOTE: This is the song of a "Whiteboy"—an agrarian revolutionist from the 1790s. The revolutionists wore white shirts over their heads.]

JOSEPH CAMPBELL (1879–1944)

Three Colts Exercising in a Six-Acre

Three colts exercising in a six-acre,
A hilly sweep of unfenced grass over the road.

What a picture they make against the skyline!
Necks stretched, hocks moving royally, tails flying;
Farm-lads up, and they crouching low on their withers.

I have a journey to go —
A lawyer to see, and a paper to sign in the Tontine —
But I slacken my pace to watch them.

Butterfly in the Fields

Dallán Dé! Dallán Dé! —
Blind thing of God, why do you play?

Why do you flit about in the sun,
Darkling, painted, lovely one?

Whom do you know through shining hours?
What do you drink from secret flowers?

Are the unseen, seeing Others
Kinfolk, blessed fosterbrothers?

Whose is the burthen then you bear,
Filmy wing of the rayhot air?

Does the silk of your cast cocoon
Knit you to night more close than noon?

Fly you in tears, as Etáin flew,
Questing the king her girlhood knew?

Or drop in dream without hindsight,
Dead to the shadow, blind to light?

I am blind, and do not play —
Dallán Dé! Dallán Dé!

Blanaid's Song

Blanaid loves roses;
And Lugh who disposes
All beautiful things,
Gave her
    Roses.

All heavenly things,
Dreambegot, fairyborn,
All natural things
Of colour and savour:
(Shawls of old kings,
Ripeness of corn,
Butterfly wings,
Veined chestnut leaves,
Dark summer eves,
Moons at high morn).
He searched for a favour,
And, pondering, gave her
    Roses.

Blanaid's black head
Wears a barret of red

From Lugh's gardenlands;
Her breasts and her hands
Are burthened with
    Roses.

— So her song closes!

ETHNA CARBERY (1866–1902)

The Love-Talker

I met the Love-Talker one eve in the glen,
He was handsomer than any of our handsome young
    men,
His eyes were blacker than the sloe, his voice sweeter far
Than the crooning of old Kevin's pipes beyond in Cool-
    nagar.

I was bound for the milking with a heart fair and free —
My grief! my grief! that bitter hour drained the life from
    me;
I thought him human lover, though his lips on mine were
    cold,
And the breath of death blew keen on me within his hold.

I know not what way he came, no shadow fell behind,
But all the sighing rushes swayed beneath a faery wind,
The thrush ceased its singing, a mist crept about,
We two clung together — with the world shut out.

Beyond the ghostly mist I could hear my cattle low,
The little cow from Ballina, clean as driven snow,
The dun cow from Kerry, the roan from Inisheer,
Oh, pitiful their calling — and his whispers in my ear!

His eyes were a fire; his words were a snare;
I cried my mother's name, but no help was there;
I made the blessed Sign; then he gave a dreary moan,
A wisp of cloud went floating by, and I stood alone.

Running ever through my head, is an old-time rune —
"Who meets the Love-Talker must weave her shroud
    soon."
My mother's face is furrowed with the salt tears that fall,
But the kind eyes of my father are the saddest sight of all.

I have spun the fleecy lint, and now my wheel is still,
The linen length is woven for my shroud fine and chill,
I shall stretch me on the bed where a happy maid I lay —
Pray for the soul of Marie Og at dawning of the day!

Brian Boy Magee
(A.D. 1641)

I am Brian Boy Magee —
My father was Eoin Bán —
I was wakened from happy dreams
By the shouts of my startled clan;
And I saw through the leaping glare
That marked where our homestead stood,
My mother swing by her hair —
And my brothers lie in their blood.

In the creepy cold of the night
The pitiless wolves came down —
Red troops from that Castle grim
Guarding Knockfergus Town;
And they hacked and lashed and hewed
With musket and rope and sword,
Till my murdered kin lay thick
In pools by the Slaughter Ford.

I fought by my father's side,
And when we were fighting sore
We saw a line of their steel
With our shrieking women before;
The red-coats drove them on
To the verge of the Gobbins grey,
Hurried them — God, the sight!
As the sea foamed up for its prey.

Oh, tall were the Gobbins cliffs,
And sharp were the rocks, my woe!
And tender the limbs that met
Such terrible death below;
Mother and babe and maid
They clutched at the empty air,
With eyeballs widened in fright,
That hour of despair.

(Sleep soft in your heaving bed,
O little fair love of my heart!
The bitter oath I have sworn
Shall be of my life a part;
And for every piteous prayer
You prayed on your way to die,
May I hear an enemy plead
While I laugh and deny.)

In the dawn that was gold and red,
Ay, red as the blood-choked stream,
I crept to the perilous brink —
Dear Christ! was the night a dream?
In all the Island of Gloom
I only had life that day —
Death covered the green hill-sides,
And tossed in the Bay.

I have vowed by the pride of my sires —
By my mother's wandering ghost —
By my kinsfolk's shattered bones
Hurled on the cruel coast —
By the sweet dead face of my love,
And the wound in her gentle breast —
To follow that murderous band,
A sleuth-hound who knows no rest.

I shall go to Phelim O'Neill
With my sorrowful tale, and crave
A blue-bright blade of Spain,
In the ranks of his soldiers brave.
And God grant me the strength to wield
That shining avenger well
When the Gael shall sweep his foe
Through the yawning gates of Hell.

I am Brian Boy Magee!
And my creed is a creed of hate;
Love, Peace, I have cast aside —
But Vengeance, *Vengeance* I wait!
Till I pay back the four-fold debt
For the horrors I witnessed there,
When my brothers moaned in their blood,
And my mother swung by her hair.

EILÉAN NÍ CHUILLEANÁIN (1942–   )

Swineherd

"When all this is over," said the swineherd,
"I mean to retire, where
Nobody will ever have heard about my special skills
And conversation is mainly about the weather.

I intend to learn how to make coffee, at least as well
As the Portuguese lay-sister in the kitchen
And polish the brass fenders every day,
I want to lie awake at night
Listening to the cream crawling to the top of the jug
And the water lying soft in the cistern.

I want to see an orchard where the trees grow in straight
    lines
And the yellow fox finds shelter between the navy-blue
    trunks,
Where it gets dark early in summer
And the apple-blossom is allowed to wither on the bough."

AUSTIN CLARKE (1896–   )

A Strong Wind

All day a strong wind blew
Across the green and brown from Kerry
The leaves hurrying, two
By three, over the road, collected
In chattering groups. New berry

Dipped with old branch. Careful insects
Flew low behind their hedges.
Held back by her pretty petticoat,
Butterfly struggled. A bit of
Paper, on which a schoolgirl had written
"Máire loves Jimmy," jumped up
Into a tree. Tapping in haste,
The wind was telegraphing, hundreds
Of miles. All Ireland raced.

The Planter's Daughter

When night stirred at sea
And the fire brought a crowd in,
They say that her beauty
Was music in mouth
And few in the candlelight
Thought her too proud,
For the house of the planter
Is known by the trees.

Men that had seen her
Drank deep and were silent,
The women were speaking
Wherever she went —
As a bell that is rung
Or a wonder told shyly,
And O she was the Sunday
In every week.

[NOTE: In barren Donegal, only a planter — a man of wealth —
could afford to have trees around his house.]

Irish-American Dignitary

Glanced down at Shannon from the sky-way
With his attendant clergy, stayed night
In Dublin, but whole day with us
To find his father's cot, now dust
And rubble, bless new church, school buildings
At Glantworth, drive to Spangle Hill
And cut first sod, hear, answer, fine speeches,
Accept a learned gown, freedom
Of ancient city, so many kissing
His ring — God love him! — almost missed
The waiting liner: that day in Cork
Had scarcely time for knife and fork.

PADRAIC COLUM (1881–   )

A Drover

To Meath of the pastures,
From wet hills by the sea,
Through Leitrim and Longford,
Go my cattle and me.

I hear in the darkness
Their slipping and breathing —
I name them the by-ways
They're to pass without heeding;

Then the wet, winding roads,
Brown bogs with black water,
And my thoughts on white ships
And the King o' Spain's daughter.

O farmer, strong farmer!
You can spend at the fair,
But your face you must turn
To your crops and your care;

And soldiers, red soldiers!
You've seen many lands,
But you walk two by two,
And by captain's commands!

O the smell of the beasts,
The wet wind in the morn,
And the proud and hard earth
Never broken for corn!

And the crowds at the fair,
The herds loosened and blind,
Loud words and dark faces,
And the wild blood behind!

(O strong men with your best
I would strive breast to breast,
I could quiet your herds,
With my words, with my words!)

I will bring you, my kine,
Where there's grass to the knee,
But you'll think of scant croppings
Harsh with salt of the sea.

River-Mates

I'll be an otter, and I'll let you swim
A mate beside me; we will venture down
A deep, dark river, when the sky above
Is shut of the sun; spoilers are we,
Thick-coated; no dog's tooth can bite at our veins,
With eyes and ears of poachers; deep-earthed ones
Turned hunters; let him slip past
The little vole; my teeth are on an edge
For the King-fish of the River!

       I hold him up
The glittering salmon that smells of the sea;
I hold him high and whistle!
       Now we go
Back to our earths; we will tear and eat
Sea-smelling salmon; you will tell the cubs
I am the Booty-bringer, I am the Lord
Of the River; the deep, dark, full and flowing River!

Interior

The little moths are creeping
Across the cottage pane;
On the floor the chickens gather,
And they make talk and complain.

And she sits by the fire
Who has reared so many men;
Her voice is low like the chickens'
With the things she says again:

"The sons that come back do be restless,
They search for the thing to say;
Then they take thought like the swallows,
And the morrow brings them away.

In the old, old days upon Innish,
The fields were lucky and bright,
And if you lay down you'd be covered
By the grass of one soft night.

And doves flew with every burial
That went from Innishore —
Two white doves before the coffined —
But the doves fly no more!"

She speaks and the chickens gather,
And they make talk and complain,
While the little moths are creeping
Across the cottage pane.

·

The Poor Girl's Meditation
Translated from the Irish (17th–19th century)

I am sitting here
Since the moon rose in the night,
Kindling a fire,
And striving to keep it alight;
The folk of the house are lying
In slumber deep;
The cocks will be crowing soon:
The whole of the land is asleep.

May I never leave this world
Until my ill-luck is gone;
Till I have cows and sheep,
And the lad that I love for my own:
I would not think it long,
The night I would lie at his breast,
And the daughters of spite, after that,
Might say the thing they liked best.

Love covers up hate,
If a girl have beauty at all:
On a bed that was narrow and high,
A three-month I lie by the wall:
When I bethought on the lad

That I left on the brow of the hill,
I wept from dark until dark
And my cheeks have the tear-tracks still.

And, O, young lad that I love,
I am no mark for your scorn:
All you can say of me
Is undowered I was born:
And if I've no fortune in hand,
Nor cattle nor sheep of my own,
This I can say, O lad,
I am fitted to lie my lone.

JAMES H. COUSINS (1873–1955)

The Corncrake

I heard him faintly, far away.
   (*Break! Break! — Break! Break!*)
Calling to the dawn of day,
   "Break! Break!"

I heard him in the yellow morn
   (*Shake! Shake! — Shake! Shake!*)
Shouting thro' the rustling corn,
   "Shake! Shake!"

I heard him near where one lay dead
   (*Ache! Ache!*)
Crying among the poppies red,
   "Ache! Ache! — Ache! Ache!"

And where a solemn yew-tree waves
   (*Wake! Wake!*)
All night he shouts among the graves,
   "Wake! Wake! — Wake! Wake!"

A Curse on a Closed Gate
Translated from the Irish

Be this the fate
Of the man who would shut his gate
On the stranger, gentle or simple, early or late.

When his mouth with a day's long hunger and thirst
      would wish
For the savour of salted fish,
Let him sit and eat his fill of an empty dish.

To the man of that ilk,
Let water stand in his churn, instead of milk
That turns a calf's coat silk.

And under the gloomy night
May never a thatch made tight
Shut out the clouds from his sight.

Above the ground or below it,
Good cheer, may he never know it,
Nor a tale by the fire, nor a dance on the road, nor a song
      by a wandering poet.

Till he open his gate
To the stranger, early or late,
And turn back the stone of his fate.

GEORGE DARLEY (1795–1846)

Runilda's Chant

O'er the wild gannet's bath
Come the Norse coursers!
O'er the whale's heritance
Gloriously steering!
With beaked heads peering,
Deep-plunging, high-rearing,
Tossing their foam abroad,
Shaking white manes aloft,
Creamy-necked, pitchy ribbed,
Steeds of the Ocean!

O'er the Sun's mirror green
Come the Norse coursers!
Trampling its glassy breadth
Into bright fragments!
Hollow-backed, huge-bosomed,
Fraught with mailed riders,
Clanging with hauberks,
Shield, spear, and battleaxe.
Canvas-winged, cable-reined,
Steeds of the Ocean!

O'er the Wind's ploughing-field
Come the Norse coursers!
By a hundred each ridden,
To the bloody feast bidden,
They rush in their fierceness
And ravine all round them!
Their shoulders enriching
With fleecy-light plunder,
Fire-spreading, foe-spurning,
Steeds of the Ocean!

THOMAS DAVIS (1814–1845)

Lament for the Death of Eoghan Ruadh O'Neill

Time: 10 November 1649. Scene: Ormond's Camp, Co. Waterford.
Speakers: a Veteran of Eoghan O'Neill's clan, and one of the horse-
men just arrived with an account of his death.

"Did they dare, did they dare, to slay Eoghan Ruadh
O'Neill?"
"Yes, they slew with poison him they feared to meet with
steel."
"May God wither up their hearts! May their blood cease
to flow!
May they walk in living death, who poisoned Eoghan
Ruadh!

"Though it break my heart to hear, say again the bitter
words."
"From Derry, against Cromwell, he marched to measure
swords;
But the weapon of the Saxon met him on his way,
And he died at Cloch Uachtar, upon Saint Leonard's
day."

Wail, wail ye for the Mighty One! Wail, wail ye for the
Dead;
Quench the hearth, and hold the breath — with ashes
strew the head.
How tenderly we loved him! How deeply we deplore!
Holy Saviour! but to think we shall never see him more!

"Sagest in the council was he, kindest in the Hall:
Sure we never won a battle — 'twas Eoghan won them all.
Had he lived — had he lived — our dear country had been
free;
But he's dead, but he's dead, and 'tis slaves we'll ever be.

"O'Farrell and Clanricarde, Preston and Red Hugh,
Audley and MacMahon—ye are valiant, wise, and true;
But—what, what are ye all to our darling who is gone?
The Rudder of our ship was he, our Castle's corner-
 stone!

"Wail, wail him through the Island! Weep, weep for our
 pride!
Would that on the battle-field our gallant chief had died!
Weep the Victor of Benburb—weep him, young man and
 old;
Weep for him, ye women—your Beautiful lies cold!

"We thought you would not die—we were sure you would
 not go,
And leave us in our utmost need to Cromwell's cruel
 blow—
Sheep without a sheperd, when the snow shuts out the
 sky—
Oh! why did you leave us, Eoghan? Why did you die?

"Soft as woman's was your voice, O'Neill! bright was your
 eye,
Oh! why did you leave us, Eoghan? why did you die?
Your troubles are all over, you're at rest with God on
 high;
But we're slaves, and we're orphans, Eoghan!—why did
 you die?"

[*Eoghan Ruadh:* Red-haired Owen]

C. DAY LEWIS (1904–   )

Jig

That winter love spoke and we raised no objection, at
Easter 'twas daisies all light and affectionate,
June sent us crazy for natural selection—not
Four traction-engines could tear us apart.
Autumn then coloured the map of our land,
Oaks shuddered and apples came ripe to the hand,
In the gap of the hills we played happily, happily,
Even the moon couldn't tell us apart.

Grave winter drew near and said, "This will not do at all—
If you continue, I fear you will rue it all."
So at the New Year we vowed to eschew it
Although we both knew it would break our heart.
But spring made hay of our good resolutions—
Lovers, you may be as wise as Confucians,
Yet once love betrays you he plays you and plays you
Like fishes for ever, so take it to heart.

LORD DUNSANY (1878–1957)

A Call to the Wild

Jimson lives in a new
  Small house where the view is shrouded
With hideous hoardings, a view
  That is every year more crowded.

Every year he is vexed
  With some new noise as a neighbour;
The tram-lines are coming next
  And the street is noisy with labour.

But one thing he sees afar,
  From a window over his back door,
Is a wood as wild as a star,
  On a hill untouched by contractor.

Thither at times, forlorn,
  From the clamour of things suburban
He turns, as the Arab at dawn
  To Mecca inclines his turban.

And this is the curious prayer
  That he prays when his heart sickens,
"Oh fox come down from your lair
  And steal our chickens."

FRANCIS A. FAHY (1845–1935)

The Queen of Connemara

Oh! my boat can swiftly float
In the teeth of wind and weather,
And outsail the fastest hooker
Between Galway and Kinsale.
When the white rim of the ocean
And the wild waves rush together —
Oh, she rides in her pride
Like a seabird in a gale.

Chorus:
She's neat, oh, she's sweet;
She's a beauty in every line —
The Queen of Connemara
Is this bounding barque of mine.

When she's loaded down with fish,
'Til the water lips the gunwale,
Not a drop she'll take aboard her
That would wash a fly away;
From the fleet she speeds out quickly
Like a greyhound from her kennel,
'Til she lands her silvery store the first
On old Kinvara Quay.

Chorus [repeat]

There's a light shines out afar
And it keeps me from dismaying —
When the clouds are ink above us,
And the sea runs white with foam,
In a cot in Connemara

There's a wife and wee ones praying
To the One Who walked the waters once
To bring us safely home.

Chorus:
She's neat, oh, she's sweet;
She's a beauty in every line —
The Queen of Connemara
Is this bounding barque of mine.

ROBERT FARREN (1909–   )

Rich Morning

This was a rich morning.

I went out and saw
spring watched-for.

I could feel the time turn round.
The trees' thought ran through me,
each one said,

"Spring's coming — that's her sky,
the sun rose *her* way
today,
that's her west wind
with the quiver in it
like young fire."

The trees were thinking
"Any moment now
she'll reach me,
and I'll blow
my buds aloud for her."

I did not hear
what water said,
and air held peace,
spring on her breast.

I turned my head
and all mirth smiled
from fine eyes.

This was a rich morning.

SIR SAMUEL FERGUSON (1810–1886)

Dear Dark Head
Translated from the Irish (17th–19th century)

Put your head, darling, darling, darling,
   Your darling black head my heart above;
Oh, mouth of honey, with the thyme for fragrance,
   Who, with heart in breast, could deny you love?

Oh, many and many a young girl for me is pining,
   Letting her locks of gold to the cold wind free,
For me, the foremost of our gay young fellows;
   But I'd leave a hundred, pure love, for thee!

Then put your head, darling, darling, darling,
  Your darling black head my heart above;
Oh, mouth of honey, with the thyme for fragrance,
  Who, with heart in breast, could deny you love?

Cashel of Munster
Translated from the Irish (17th–18th century)

I'd wed you without herds, without money, or rich array,
And I'd wed you on a dewy morning at day-dawn grey;
My bitter woe it is, love, that we are not far away
In Cashel town, though the bare deal board were our mar-
    riage bed this day!

Oh, fair maid, remember the green hillside,
Remember how I hunted about the valleys wide;
Time now has worn me; my locks are turned to grey,
The year is scarce and I am poor, but send me not, love,
    away!

Oh, deem not my blood is of base strain, my girl,
Oh, deem not my birth was as the birth of the churl;
Marry me, and prove me, and say soon you will,
That noble blood is written on my right side still!

My purse holds no red gold, no coin of the silver white,
No herds are mine to drive through the long twilight!
But the pretty girl that would take me, all bare though I
    be and lone,
Oh, I'd take her with me kindly to the county Tyrone.

Oh, my girl, I can see 'tis in trouble you are,
And, oh, my girl, I see 'tis your people's reproach you bear:
"I am a girl in trouble for his sake with whom I fly,
And, oh, may no other maiden know such reproach as I!"

PADRAIC FIACC (1924–   )

Deranged

Liefer would I turn and love
The ox in the by-path, the sloe on the bush
Than take to the blithe creature would crush
    All in her hands!

It is fitting not for a young man
To turning of face backward like this
Carrying a cut from the knife of her kiss,
    The smart of her lips!

O comely indeed the arrangement of her hair!
Beyond that the ease of her shoulder,
Her two blue eyes: nothing bolder!
    Her two blue eyes!

O moonlight that wasted me, O harsh little stars:
Sharp cutting reproaches from what tongue could not say!
She left me alone one scald of a day,
    The deceit of the one!

Liefer would I turn and love
The ox in the by-path, the barnyard dove!

The Boy and the Geese

The swans rise up with their wings in day
And they fly to the sky like the clouds away;

Yet with all their beauty and grace and might
I would rather have geese for their less-smooth flight.

I would rather have geese for they're ugly like me
And because they are ugly, as ugly can be
I would rather have geese for their mystery.

ROBIN FLOWER (1881–1946)

Pangur Bán
Translated from the Irish (9th century)

I and Pangur Bán, my cat,
'Tis a like task we are at;
Hunting mice is his delight,
Hunting words I sit all night.

Better far than praise of men
'Tis to sit with book and pen;
Pangur bears me no ill will,
He too plies his simple skill.

'Tis a merry thing to see
At our tasks how glad are we,
When at home we sit and find
Entertainment to our mind.

Oftentimes a mouse will stray
In the hero Pangur's way;
Oftentimes my keen thought set
Takes a meaning in its net.

'Gainst the wall he sets his eye
Full and fierce and sharp and sly;
'Gainst the wall of knowledge I
All my little wisdom try.

When a mouse darts from its den,
O how glad is Pangur then!
O what gladness do I prove
When I solve the doubts I love!

So in peace our tasks we ply,
Pangur Bán, my cat and I;
In our hearts we find our bliss,
I have mine and he has his.

Practice every day has made
Pangur perfect in his trade;
I get wisdom day and night
Turning darkness into light.

[NOTE: *Pangur Bán* is pronounced Bangur Bawn.]

He That Never Read a Line
Translated from the Irish (9th century)

'Tis sad to see the sons of learning
In everlasting Hellfire burning
While he that never read a line
Doth in eternal glory shine.

The Passage at Night — The Blaskets

The dark cliff towered up to the stars that flickered
And seemed no more than lights upon its brow,
And on the slippery quay
Men talked — a rush of Gaelic never-ending.
I stepped down to the boat,
A frail skin rocking on the unquiet water,
And at a touch she trembled
And skimmed out lightly to the moonlit seaway.
I lying in the stern
Felt all the tremble of water slipping under,
As wave on wave lifted and let us down.

The water from the oars dripped fiery; burning
With a dull glow great globes
Followed the travelling blades. A voice rose singing
To the tune of the running water and loud oars:
"I met a maiden in the misty morning,
And she was barefooted under rippling tresses.
I asked her was she Helen, was she Deirdre?
She answered: 'I am none of these but Ireland.
Men have died for me, men have still to die.'"
The voice died then, and, growing in the darkness,
The shape of the Great Island
Rose up out of the water hugely glooming,
And wearing lights like stars upon its brow.

PERCY FRENCH (1854–1922)

The Mountains of Mourne

Oh, Mary, this London's a wonderful sight,
Wid the people here workin' by day and by night:
   They don't sow potatoes, nor barley, nor wheat,
   But there's gangs o' them diggin' for gold in the street—
At least, when I axed them, that's what I was told,
So I just took a hand at this diggin' for gold,
   But for all that I found there, I might as well be
   Where the Mountains o' Mourne sweep down to the
     sea.

I believe that, when writin', a wish you expressed
As to how the fine ladies in London were dressed.
   Well, if you'll believe me, when axed to a ball,
   They don't wear a top to their dresses at all!

Oh, I've seen them meself, and you could not, in thrath,
Say if they were bound for a ball or a bath —
   Don't be startin' them fashions now, Mary Machree,
   Where the Mountains o' Mourne sweep down to the
   sea

I seen England's King from the top of a 'bus —
I never knew him, though he means to know us:
   And though by the Saxon we once were oppressed,
   Still, I cheered — God forgive me — I cheered wid the
   rest.
And now that he's visited Erin's green shore,
We'll be much better friends than we've been heretofore,
   When we've got all we want, we're as quiet as can be
   Where the Mountains o' Mourne sweep down to the
   sea.

You remember young Peter O'Loughlin, of course —
Well, here he is now at the head o' the Force.
   I met him today, I was crossin' the Strand,
   And he stopped the whole street wid wan wave of his
   hand:
And there we stood talking of days that are gone,
While the whole population of London looked on;
   But for all these great powers, he's wishful like me,
   To be back where dark Mourne sweeps down to the
   sea.

There's beautiful girls here — oh, never mind!
With beautiful shapes Nature never designed,
   And lovely complexions, all roses and crame,
   But O'Loughlin remarked wid regard to them same:
"That if at those roses you venture to sip,
The colour might all come away on your lip,"
   So I'll wait for the wild rose that's waitin' for me —
   Where the Mountains o' Mourne sweep down to the
   sea.

Come Back, Paddy Reilly

The Garden of Eden has vanished they say,
But I know the lie of it still.
Just turn to the left at the bridge of Finea,
And stop when half-way to Cootehill.
'Tis there I will find it, I know sure enough,
When fortune has come to my call.
Oh, the grass it is green around Ballyjamesduff,
And the blue sky is over it all!
And tones that are tender and tones that are gruff
Are whispering over the sea,
"Come back, Paddy Reilly, to Ballyjamesduff,
Come home, Paddy Reilly, to me."

My Mother once told me that when I was born,
The day that I first saw the light,
I looked down the street on that very first morn
And gave a great crow of delight.
Now most new-born babies appear in a huff
And start with a sorrowfull squall,
But I knew I was born in Ballyjamesduff
And that's why I smiled on them all!
The baby's a man now, he's toil-worn and tough,
Still, whispers come over the sea,
"Come back, Paddy Reilly, to Ballyjamesduff,
 Come home, Paddy Reilly, to me."

The night that we danced by the light o' the moon,
Wid Phil to the fore wid his flute,
When Phil threw his lip over "Come agin soon,"
He'd dance the foot out o' yer boot!
The day that I took long Magee by the scruff,
For slanderin' Rosie Kilrain;

Then marchin' him straight out of Ballyjamesduff,
Assisted him into a drain.
Oh! sweet are me dreams as the dudeen I puff,
Of whisperings over the sea:
"Come back, Paddy Reilly, to Ballyjamesduff,
Come home, Paddy Reilly, to me."

MONK GIBBON (1896–   )

The Discovery

Adam, who thought himself immortal still,
Though cast from Eden, not knowing yet of death,
Nor guessing that what has beginning ends,
Nor that the life goes also with the breath,

Wandering to the empty fields one day,
Pushing the grass aside, finds Abel slain,
His arms thrown out, his head with briars twined,
And on the ground beside a dull red stain.

"Abel, it is not time for sleeping now;
Have you forgot the curse upon us put?"
So, standing by his side, he gazes down.
Thinking he jests, he stirs him with his foot.

Silence, no sound at all, a breathless calm;
The warm day sighs; its sighing does not last.
The grass-tops quiver slightly; through the grass
A small field-mouse, disturbed, goes hurrying past.

Then, seized with sudden fear, he flings himself
Beside the corpse, cries, "For your mother's sake
Give me an answer." Still no answer comes,
Only the cry, "Abel, awake, awake!"

I Tell Her She Is Lovely . . .

I tell her she is lovely, and she laughs,
Shy laughter altogether lovely too,
Knowing, perhaps, that it was true before,
And, when she laughs, that it is still more true.

OLIVER ST. JOHN GOGARTY (1878–1957)

O Boys! O Boys!

O Boys, the times I've seen!
The things I've done and known!
If you knew where I have been?
Or half the joys I've had,
You never would leave me alone;
But pester me to tell,
Swearing to keep it dark,
What . . . but I know quite well:
Every solicitor's clerk
Would break out and go mad;
And all the dogs would bark!

There was a young fellow of old
Who spoke of a wonderful town,
Built on a lake of gold,
With many a barge and raft
Afloat in the cooling sun,
And lutes upon the lake
Played by such courtesans . . .
The sight was enough to take
The reason out of a man's
Brain; and to leave him daft,
Babbling of lutes and fans.

The tale was right enough:
Willows and orioles,
And ladies skilled in love:
But they listened only to smirk,
For he spoke to incredulous fools,
And, maybe, was sorry he spoke;
For no one believes in joys,
And Peace on Earth is a joke,
Which, anyhow, telling destroys;
So better go on with your work:
But Boys! O Boys! O Boys!

Back from the Country

Back from the country
Ruddy as an apple,
Looking ripe and rural
As the maid a farmer seeks;
Fresh as an apple
Shining in the pantry,
Back you came to Dublin
Whom I had not seen for weeks:
How I hid my laughter
Fearing to offend you,
Back from the country
With your apple cheeks!

ALFRED PERCEVAL GRAVES (1846–1931)

Herring Is King

Let all the fish that swim the sea,
   Salmon and turbot, cod and ling,
Bow down the head, and bend the knee
   To herring, their king! to herring, their king!
Sing, Hugamar féin an sowra lin'
'Tis we have brought the summer in.

The sun sank down so round and red
   Upon the bay, upon the bay;
The sails shook idle overhead,
   Becalmed we lay, becalmed we lay;
Sing, Hugamar féin an sowra lin'
'Tis we have brought the summer in.

Till Shawn, the Eagle, dropped on deck —
   The bright-eyed boy, the bright-eyed boy;
'Tis he has spied your silver track,
   Herring, our joy — herring, our joy;
Sing, Hugamar féin an sowra lin'
'Tis we have brought the summer in.

It was in with the sails and away to shore
   With the rise and swing, the rise and swing
Of two stout lads at each smoking oar,
   After herring, our king — herring, our king;
Sing, Hugamar féin an sowra lin'
'Tis we have brought the summer in.

The Manx and the Cornish raised the shout,
   And joined the chase, and joined the chase;
But their fleets they fouled as they went about,
   And we won the race, we won the race.
Sing, Hugamar féin an sowra lin'
'Tis we have brought the summer in.

For we turned and faced you full to land,
    Down the goleen long, the goleen long,
And after you slipped from strand to strand
    Our nets so strong, our nets so strong;
Sing, Hugamar féin an sowra lin'
'Tis we have brought the summer in.

Then we called to our sweethearts and our wives
    "Come welcome us home, welcome us home!"
Till they ran to meet us for their lives
    Into the foam, into the foam;
Sing, Hugamar féin an sowra lin'
'Tis we have brought the summer in.

O the kissing of hands and waving of caps
    From girl and boy, from girl and boy,
While you leaped by scores in the lasses' laps,
    Herring, our pride and joy;
Sing, Hugamar féin an sowra lin'
'Tis we have brought the summer in.

[*goleen:* a small rocky inlet]

Father O'Flynn

Of priests we can offer a charmin' variety,
Far renowned for larnin' and piety:
Still, I'd advance you, widout impropriety,
    Father O'Flynn as the flower of them all.

Chorus:
Here's a health to you, Father O'Flynn,
Slainte, and slainte, and slainte agin:
  Powerfulest preacher, and
  Tinderest teacher, and
Kindliest creature in ould Donegal.

Don't talk of your Provost and Fellows of Trinity,
Famous for ever at Greek and Latinity,
Dad and the divels and all at Divinity,
  Father O'Flynn'd makes hares of them all.
    Come, I vinture to give you my word,
    Never the likes of his logic was heard
      Down from Mythology
      Into Thayology,
    Troth! and Conchology, if he'd the call.

Chorus [repeat]

Och! Father O'Flynn, you've the wonderful way wid you,
All ould sinners are wishful to pray wid you,
All the young childer are wild for to play wid you,
  You've such a way wid you, Father avick!
    Still, for all you've so gentle a soul,
    Gad, you've your flock in the grandest conthroul:
      Checking the crazy ones,
      Coaxin' onaisy ones,
    Liftin' the lazy ones on wid the stick.

Chorus [repeat]

And though quite avoidin' all foolish frivolity,
Still at all seasons of innocent jollity,

Where was the playboy could claim an equality
At comicality, Father, wid you?
Once the Bishop looked grave at your jest,
Till this remark set him off wid the rest:
"Is it lave gaiety
All to the laity?
Cannot the clargy be Irishmen too?"

Chorus:
Here's a health to you, Father O'Flynn
Slainte, and slainte, and slainte agin:
Powerfulest preacher, and
Tinderest teacher, and
Kindliest creature in ould Donegal.

LADY GREGORY (1852–1932)

Donal Oge: Grief of a Girl's Heart
Translated from the Irish (*19th century*)

O Donal Oge, if you go across the sea,
Bring myself with you and do not forget it;
And you will have a sweetheart for fair days and market
days,
And the daughter of the King of Greece beside you at
night.

It is late last night the dog was speaking of you;
The snipe was speaking of you in her deep marsh.
It is you are the lonely bird through the woods;
And that you may be without a mate until you find me.

[*Donal Oge:* Young Donal]

You promised me, and you said a lie to me,
That you would be before me where the sheep are flocked;
I gave a whistle and three hundred cries to you,
And I found nothing there but a bleating lamb.

You promised me a thing that was hard for you,
A ship of gold under a silver mast;
Twelve towns with a market in all of them,
And a fine white court by the side of the sea.

You promised me a thing that is not possible,
That you would give me gloves of the skin of a fish;
That you would give me shoes of the skin of a bird;
And a suit of the dearest silk in Ireland.

O Donal Oge, it is I would be better to you
Than a high, proud, spendthrift lady:
I would milk the cow; I would bring help to you;
And if you were hard pressed, I would strike a blow for
    you.

O, ochone, and it's not with hunger
Or with wanting food, or drink, or sleep,
That I am growing thin, and my life is shortened;
But it is the love of a young man has withered me away.

It is early in the morning that I saw him coming,
Going along the road on the back of a horse;
He did not come to me; he made nothing of me;
And it is on my way home that I cried my fill.

When I go by myself to the Well of Loneliness,
I sit down and I go through my trouble;
When I see the world and do not see my boy,
He that has an amber shade in his hair.

It was on that Sunday I gave my love to you;
The Sunday that is last before Easter Sunday.
And myself on my knees reading the Passion;
And my two eyes giving love to you for ever.

O, aya! my mother, give myself to him;
And give him all that you have in the world;
Get out yourself to ask for alms,
And do not come back and forward looking for me.

My mother said to me not to be talking with you, today,
Or tomorrow, or on Sunday;
It was a bad time she took for telling me that;
It was shutting the door after the house was robbed.

My heart is as black as the blackness of the sloe,
Or as the black coal that is on the smith's forge;
Or as the sole of a shoe left in white halls;
It was you put that darkness over my life.

You have taken the east from me; you have taken the west
    from me,
You have taken what is before me and what is behind me;
You have taken the moon, you have taken the sun from
    me,
And my fear is great that you have taken God from me!

SEAMUS HEANEY (1939–   )

The Forge

All I know is a door into the dark.
Outside, old axles and iron hoops rusting;
Inside, the hammered anvil's short-pitched ring,
The unpredictable fantail of sparks
Or hiss when a new shoe toughens in water.
The anvil must be somewhere in the center,
Horned as a unicorn, at one end square,
Set there immoveable: an altar
Where he expends himself in shape and music.
Sometimes, leather-aproned, hairs in his nose,
He leans out on the jamb, recalls a clatter
Of hoofs where traffic is flashing in rows;
Then grunts and goes in, with a slam and flick
To beat real iron out, to work the bellows.

Follower

My father worked with a horse plough,
His shoulders globed like a full sail strung
Between the shafts and the furrow.
The horses strained at his clicking tongue.

An expert. He would set the wing
And fit the bright steel-pointed sock.
The sod rolled over without breaking.
At the headrig, with a single pluck

Of reins, the sweating team turned round
And back into the land. His eye
Narrowed and angled at the ground,
Mapping the furrow exactly.

I stumbled in his hob-nailed wake,
Fell sometimes on the polished sod;
Sometimes he rode me on his back
Dipping and rising to his plod.

I wanted to grow up and plough,
To close one eye, stiffen my arm.
All I ever did was follow
In his broad shadow round the farm.

I was a nuisance, tripping, falling,
Yapping always. But today
It is my father who keeps stumbling
Behind me, and will not go away.

JOHN HEWITT (1907–   )

O Country People

O country people, you of the hill farms,
huddled so in darkness I cannot tell
whether the light across the glen is a star,
or the bright lamp spilling over the sill,
I would be neighbourly, would come to terms
with your existence, but you are so far;
there is a wide bog between us, a high wall.
I've tried to learn the smaller parts of speech
in your slow language, but my thoughts need more
flexible shapes to move in, if I am to reach
into the hearth's red heart across the half-door.

You are coarse to my senses, to my washed skin;
I shall maybe learn to wear dung on my heels,
but the slow assurance, the unconscious discipline
informing your vocabulary of skill,
is beyond my mastery, who have followed a trade
three generations now, at counter and desk;
hand me a rake, and I, at once, betrayed,
will shed more sweat than is needed for the task.

If I could gear my mind to the year's round
take season into season without a break,
instead of feeling my heart bound and rebound
because of the full moon or the first snowflake,
I should have gained something. Your secret is pace.
Already in your company I can keep step,
but alone, involved in a headlong race,
I never know the moment when to stop.

I know the level you accept me on,
like a strange bird observed about the house,
or sometimes seen out flying on the moss,
that may, tomorrow, or next week, be gone,
liable to return without warning
on a May afternoon and away in the morning.

But we are no part of your world, your way,
as a field or a tree is, or a spring well.
We are not held to you by mesh of kin;
we must always take a step back to begin,
and there are so many things you never tell
because we would not know the things you say.

I recognize the limits I can stretch;
even a lifetime among you should leave me strange,
for I would not change enough, and you will not change;
there'd still be strata neither'd ever reach.
And so I cannot ever hope to become,
for all my goodwill towards you, yours to me,
even a phrase or a story that will come
pat to the tongue, part of the tapestry
of apt response, at the appropriate time,
like a wise saw, a joke, an ancient rime
used when the last stack's topped at the day's end,
or when the last lint's carted round the bend.

In This Year of Grace

The night-sky red, crackle and roar of flame,
the barricades across the ruined street,
the thump of stones, the shots, the thudding feet;
as mob greets mob with claim and counterclaim,
each blames the other, none accepts the blame,
for fears entrenched will not permit retreat,
when creed and creed inhospitably meet,
and each child's fate foreshadowed in its name.

So fare our cities in this year of grace,
sick with old poisons seeped from history;
frustration on one side, the other fear
sodden with guilt. To their embattled place
the stubborn masters cling, while year by year
from this infection no man's blood runs free.

[NOTE: Written after the Belfast riots in the summer of 1969]

F. R. HIGGINS (1896–1941)

Padraic O'Conaire, Gaelic Storyteller

They've paid the last respects in sad tobacco
And silent is this wakehouse in its haze;
They've paid the last respects; and now their whiskey
Flings laughing words on mouths of prayer and praise;
And so young couples huddle by the gables,
O let them grope home through the hedgy night—
Alone I'll mourn my old friend, while the cold dawn
Thins out the holy candlelight.

Respects are paid to one loved by the people;
Ah, was he not—among our mighty poor—
The sudden wealth cast on those pools of darkness,
Those bearing, just, a star's faint signature;
And so he was to me, close friend, near brother,
Dear Padraic of the wide and sea-cold eyes—
So lovable, so courteous and noble,
The very West was in his soft replies.

They'll miss his heavy stick and stride in Wicklow—
His story-talking down Winetavern Street,
Where old men sitting in the wizen daylight
Have kept an edge upon his gentle wit;
While women on the grassy streets of Galway,
Who hearken for his passing—but in vain,
Shall hardly tell his step as shadows vanish
Through archways of forgotten Spain.

Ah, they'll say: Padraic's gone again exploring;
But now down glens of brightness, O he'll find
An alehouse overflowing with wise Gaelic
That's braced in vigour by the bardic mind,
And there his thoughts shall find their own forefathers—

In minds to whom our heights of race belong,
In crafty men, who ribbed a ship or turned
The secret joinery of song.

Alas, death mars the parchment of his forehead;
And yet for him, I know, the earth is mild —
The windy fidgets of September grasses
Can never tease a mind that loved the wild;
So drink his peace — this grey juice of the barley
Runs with a light that ever pleased his eye —
While old flames nod and gossip on the hearthstone
And only the young winds cry.

Father and Son

Only last week, walking the hushed fields
Of our most lovely Meath, now thinned by November,
I came to where the road from Laracor leads
To the Boyne river — that seemed more lake than river,
Stretched in uneasy light and stript of reeds.

And walking longside an old weir
Of my people's, where nothing stirs — only the shadowed
Leaden flight of a heron up the lean air —
I went unmanly with grief, knowing how my father,
Happy though captive in years, walked last with me there.

Yes, happy in Meath with me for a day
He walked, taking stock of herds hid in their own breath-
    ing;
And naming colts, gusty as wind, once steered by his hand,
Lightnings winked in the eyes that were half shy in greet-
    ing
Old friends — the wild blades, when he gallivanted the
    land.

For that proud, wayward man now my heart breaks—
Breaks for the man whose mind was a secret eyrie,
Whose kind hand was sole signet of his race,
Who curbed me, scorned my green ways, yet increasingly
   loved me
Till Death drew its grey blind down his face.

And yet I am pleased that even my reckless ways
Are living shades of his rich calms and passions—
Witnesses for him and for those faint namesakes
With whom now he is one, under yew branches,
Yes, one in a graven silence no bird breaks.

At Flock Mass

I only knew her as a spouse
Whose match with me enlarged my herd;
—A wife well mated to the house,

So mild in movement, soft in word,
That who would heed her in the room
At hearth or needle, bread or broom?

But yesterday at Galway sports,
In a drinking-tent, a man told me
Of beauties handled in Spanish ports;
"Yet cross-eyed would they seem," said he,
"Near one outside, whose look cowed mine
And she demurely sipping wine.

Have you not seen her, O, her mouth:
A bud, maybe—the flower's hint;
Unfathomed wells from nights of drought
Have filled her eyes; and what a dint
Between each snowy breast, each limb—
As if a neat breeze moulded them."

And so I listened till he said,
"O there she is!" Then, on my life,
I thought the drink had turned his head
To throw such beauty on my wife!
But there, by hell, I see it's true—
Just look at her tip to her pew!

She genuflects; and our new priest
Looks—only to falter in the Mass;
Even the altar boy has ceased
And his responses, now, alas,
Are not "amen"—but towards the door
He seems to sigh: *a stoir, a stoir.*

[*a stoir:* my treasure]

DOUGLAS HYDE (1860–1946)

Ringleted Youth of My Love
Translated from the Irish (19th century)

Ringleted youth of my love,
  With thy locks bound loosely behind thee,
You passed by the road above,
  But you never came in to find me;
Where were the harm for you
  If you came for a little to see me;
Your kiss is a wakening dew
  Were I ever so ill or so dreamy.

If I had golden store
  I would make a nice little boreen
To lead straight up to his door,
  The door of the house of my storeen;
Hoping to God not to miss
  The sound of his footfall in it,
I have waited so long for his kiss
  That for days I have slept not a minute.

I thought, O my love! you were so —
  As the moon is, or sun on a fountain,
And I thought after that you were snow,
  The cold snow on top of the mountain;
And I thought after that you were more
  Like God's lamp shining to find me,
Or the bright star of knowledge before,
  And the star of knowledge behind me.

You promised me high-heeled shoes,
  And satin and silk, my storeen,

[*boreen:* lane]

And to follow me, never to lose,
  Though the ocean were round us roaring;
Like a bush in a gap in a wall
  I am now left lonely without thee,
And this house, I grow dead of, is all
  That I see around or about me.

Bruadar and Smith and Glinn
Translated from the Irish

Bruadar and Smith and Glinn,
  Amen, dear God, I pray,
May they lie low in waves of woe,
  And tortures slow each day!
      Amen!

Bruadar and Smith and Glinn
  Helpless and cold, I pray,
Amen! I pray, O King,
  To see them pine away.
      Amen!

Bruadar and Smith and Glinn
  May flails of sorrow flay!
Cause for lamenting, snares and cares
  Be theirs by night and day!
      Amen!

Blindness come down on Smith,
  Palsy on Bruadar come,
Amen, O King of Brightness! Smite
  Glinn in his members numb,
      Amen!

Smith in the pangs of pain,
  Stumbling on Bruadar's path,
King of the Elements, Oh, Amen!
  Let loose on Glinn Thy Wrath.
        Amen!

For Bruadar gape the grave,
  Up-shovel for Smith the mould,
Amen, O King of the Sunday! Leave
  Glinn in the devil's hold.
        Amen!

Terrors on Bruadar rain,
  And pain upon pain on Glinn,
Amen, O King of the Stars! And Smith
  May the devil be linking him.
        Amen!

Glinn in a shaking ague,
  Cancer on Bruadar's tongue,
Amen, O King of the Heavens! and Smith
  Forever stricken dumb.
        Amen!

Thirst but no drink for Glinn,
  Smith in a cloud of grief,
Amen! O King of the Saints; and rout
  Bruadar without relief.
        Amen!

Smith without child or heir,
  And Bruadar bare of store,
Amen, O King of the Friday! Tear
  For Glinn his black heart's core.
        Amen!

Bruadar with nerveless limbs,
　Hemp strangling Glinn's last breath,
Amen, O King of the World's Light!
　And Smith in grips with death.
　　　　Amen!

Glinn stiffening for the tomb,
　Smith wasting to decay,
Amen, O King of the Thunder's gloom,
　And Bruadar sick alway.
　　　　Amen!

Smith like a sieve of holes,
　Bruadar with throat decay,
Amen, O King of the Orders! Glinn
　A buck-show every day.
　　　　Amen!

Hell-hounds to hunt for Smith,
　Glinn led to hang on high,
Amen, O King of the Judgment Day!
　And Bruadar rotting by.
　　　　Amen!

Curses on Glinn, I cry,
　My curse on Bruadar be,
Amen, O King of the Heavens high!
　Let Smith in bondage be.
　　　　Amen!

Showers of want and blame,
　Reproach, and shame of face,
Smite them all three, and smite again,
　Amen, O King of Grace!
　　　　Amen!

Melt, may the three, away,
   Bruadar and Smith and Glinn,
Fall in a swift and sure decay
   And lose, but never win.
         Amen!

May pangs pass through thee, Smith,
   (Let the wind not take my prayer),
May I see before the year is out
   Thy heart's blood flowing there.
         Amen!

Leave Smith no place nor land,
   Let Bruadar wander wide,
May the Devil stand at Glinn's right hand,
   And Glinn to him be tied.
         Amen!

All ill from every airt
   Come down upon the three,
And blast them ere the year be out
   In rout and misery.
         Amen!

Glinn let misfortune bruise,
   Bruadar lose blood and brains,
Amen, O Jesus! hear my voice,
   Let Smith be bent in chains.
         Amen!

I accuse both Glinn and Bruadar,
   And Smith I accuse to God,
May a breach and a gap be upon the three,
   And the Lord's avenging rod.
         Amen!

Each one of the wicked three
  Who raised against me their hand,
May fire from heaven come down and slay
  This day their perjured band,
            Amen!

May none of their race survive,
  May God destroy them all,
Each curse of the psalms in the holy books
  Of the prophets upon them fall.
            Amen!

Blight skull, and ear, and skin,
  And hearing, and voice, and sight,
Amen! before the year be out,
  Blight, Son of the Virgin, blight.
            Amen!

May my curses hot and red
  And all I have said this day,
Strike the Black Peeler, too,
  Amen, dear God, I pray!
            Amen!

[NOTE: A Peeler is a policeman.]

VALENTIN IREMONGER (1918–   )

Spring Stops Me Suddenly

Spring stops me suddenly like ground
Glass under a door, squeaking and gibbering.
I put my hand to my cheek and the tips
Of my fingers feel blood pulsing and quivering.

A bud on a branch brushes the back
Of my hand and I look, without moving, down.
Summer is there, screwed and fused, compressed,
Neat as a bomb, its casing a dull brown.

From the window of a farther tree I hear
A chirp and a twitter; I blink.
A tow-headed vamp of a finch on a branch
Cocks a roving eye, tips me the wink.

And, instantly, the whole great hot-lipped ensemble
Of birds and birds, of clay and glass doors,
Reels in with its ragtime chorus, staggering
The theme of the time, a jam-session's rattle and roar.

With drums of summer jittering in the background
Dully and, deeper down and more human, the sobbing
Oboes of autumn falling across the track of the tune,
Winter's furtive bassoon like a sea-lion snorting and
    bobbing.

There is something here I do not get,
Some menace that I do not comprehend,
Yet, so intoxicating is the song,
I cannot follow its thought right to the end.

So up the garden path I go with Spring
Promising sacks and robes to rig my years
And a young girl to gladden my heart in a tartan
Scarf and freedom from my facile fears.

This Houre Her Vigill . . .

Elizabeth, frigidly stretched,
On a spring day surprised us
With her starched dignity and the quietness
Of her hands clasping a black cross.

With book and candle and holy-water dish
She received us in the room with the blind down.
Her eyes were peculiarly closed and we knelt shyly,
Noticing the blot of her hair on the white pillow.

We met that evening by the crumbling wall
In the field behind the house where I lived
And talked it over but could find no reason
Why she had left us whom she had liked so much.

Death, yes, we understood: something to do
With age and decay, decrepit bodies.
But here was this vigorous one aloof and prim
Who would not answer our furtive whispers.

Next morning, hearing the priest call her name,
I fled outside, being full of certainty,
And cried my seven years against the church's stone wall.
For eighteen years I did not speak her name.

Until this autumn day when, in a gale,
A sapling fell outside my window, its branches
Rebelliously blotting the lawn's green. Suddenly, I
    thought
Of Elizabeth, frigidly stretched.

PATRICK KAVANAGH (1905–1967)

To a Late Poplar

Not yet half-drest
O tardy bride!
And the priest
And the bridegroom and the guests
Have been waiting a full hour.

The meadow choir
Is playing the wedding march
Two fields away,
And squirrels are already leaping in ecstasy
Among leaf-full branches.

Inniskeen Road: July Evening

The bicycles go by in twos and threes —
There's a dance in Billy Brennan's barn tonight,
And there's the half-talk code of mysteries
And the wink-and-elbow language of delight.
Half-past eight and there is not a spot
Upon a mile of road, no shadow thrown
That might turn out a man or woman, not
A footfall tapping secrecies of stone.

I have what every poet hates in spite
Of all the solemn talk of contemplation.
Oh, Alexander Selkirk knew the plight
Of being king and government and nation.
A road, a mile of kingdom, I am king
Of banks and stones and every blooming thing.

Pegasus

My soul was an old horse
Offered for sale in twenty fairs.
I offered him to the Church — the buyers
Were little men who feared his unusual airs.
One said: "Let him remain unbid
In the wind and rain and hunger
Of sin and we will get him —
With the winkers thrown in — for nothing."

Then the men of State looked at
What I'd brought for sale.
One minister, wondering if
Another horse-body would fit the tail
That he'd kept for sentiment —

The relic of his own soul—
Said, "I will graze him in lieu of his labour."
I lent him for a week or more
And he came back a hurdle of bones,
Starved, overworked, in despair.
I nursed him on the roadside grass
To shape him for another fair.

I lowered my price. I stood him where
The broken-winded, spavined stand
And crooked shopkeepers said that he
Might do a season on the land—
But not for high-paid work in towns.
He'd do a tinker, possibly.
I begged, "O make some offer now,
A soul is a poor man's tragedy.
He'll draw your dungiest cart," I said,
"Show you short cuts to Mass,
Teach weather lore, at night collect
Bad debts from poor men's grass."
        And they would not.

    Where the
Tinkers quarrel I went down
With my horse, my soul.
I cried, "Who will bid me half a crown?"
From their rowdy bargaining
Not one turned. "Soul," I prayed,
"I have hawked you through the world
Of Church and State and meanest trade.
But this evening, halter off,
Never again will it go on.
On the south side of ditches
There is grazing of the sun.
No more haggling with the world. . . ."

As I said these words he grew
Wings upon his back. Now I may ride him
Every land my imagination knew.

PEADAR KEARNEY (1883–1942)

Whack Fol the Diddle

I'll sing you a song of Peace and Love,
Whack fol the diddle lol the dido day.
To the land that reigns all lands above,
Whack fol the diddle lol the dido day.
May peace and plenty be her share,
Who kept our homes from want and care,
Oh, "God bless England" is our prayer,
Whack fol the diddle lol the dido day.

Chorus:
Whack fol the diddle lol the dido day,
So we say, Hip Hurray!
Come and listen while we pray
Whack fol the diddle lol the dido day.

When we were savage, fierce and wild,
Whack fol the diddle lol the dido day.
She came as a mother to her child,
Whack fol the diddle lol the dido day.
She gently raised us from the slime,
Kept our hands from hellish crime,
And sent us to Heaven in her own good time,
Whack fol the diddle lol the dido day.

Chorus [repeat]

Our fathers oft were naughty boys,
Whack fol the diddle lol the dido day.
Pikes and guns are dangerous toys,
Whack fol the diddle lol the dido day.
From Beal'-n-ath Buidhe to Peter's Hill

They made poor England weep her fill,
But old Britannia loves us still,
Whack fol the diddle lol the dido day.

Chorus [*repeat*]

Oh, Irishmen forget the past,
Whack fol the diddle lol the dido day.
And think of the day that is coming fast,
Whack fol the diddle lol the dido day.
When we shall all be civilized,
Neat and clean, and well advised,
Oh, won't Mother England be surprised,
Whack fol the diddle lol the dido day.

Chorus:
Whack fol the diddle lol the dido day,
So we say, Hip Hurray!
Come and listen while we pray
Whack fol the diddle lol the dido day.

[NOTE: In 1916, the time of "the troubles" in Ireland, anyone caught singing this song was subject to arrest.]

RICHARD KELL (1927–   )

Citadels

That king spent fifty years or more
Holding the devil at bay;
Work was another name for war;
But then, growing grey,
He withdrew his men,
Thought the devil would scarcely
Trouble him again
Since they had fought so fiercely.
And in no time the enemy
Came swarming fresh from Hades,
Quietly took the city
And raped the golden ladies.

This one at the first surprise
Let the invaders in,
Allowed them to swank and fraternise
And soak themselves with gin;
And when they stank with pleasure,
Revealed at their most ghoulish,
Gravely took their measure
And found them rather foolish.
Disarmed them while they snored,
Prodded them back to Hades,
And feeling never so bored
Returned to his golden ladies.

The Makers

The artisan didn't collect his gear and say
"What beautiful object shall I make today?"

The poet didn't fondle a phrase and gape,
And think, "What elegant structure can I shape?"

The artisan made a gatepost
So that a certain gate could be opened and closed.

The poet started a poem
So that a meaning could reveal a form.

The gatepost is itself, sturdy and straight:
Precisely this gatepost for this gate.

The poem is itself, the form-in-content:
Exactly these words for what was meant.

The gatepost is rough, distinct and lovable,
Untouched by the purpose that made it possible.

The poem is plain, final, able to please,
Clear of the hungers that made it what it is.

BRENDAN KENNELLY (1936–   )

The Black Cliffs, Ballybunion

White horses galloping on the sand
Toss their beautiful Atlantic manes
At girls selling seagrass and
Periwinkles. Whatever pain
Is in God's heart is in the sea
That batters the black cliffs where I stand,
Aware of love's infinity
And how infinitely little I understand.
A man is carting seaweed near the rocks
Where I saw a brother and sister drown
Only three summers ago;
A curlew cries where the sea breaks, gathers, breaks;
God cries passionately to be known
But who would dare to begin to know?

Light Dying

In Memoriam Frank O'Connor (Michael O'Donovan)

Climbing the last steps to your house, I knew
That I would find you in your chair,
Watching the light die along the canal,
Recalling the glad creators, all
Who'd played a part in the miracle;
A silver-haired remembering king, superb there
In dying light, all ghosts being at your beck and call,
You made them speak as only you could do,

Of generosity or loneliness or love
Because, you said, all men are voices, heard
In the pure air of the imagination.
I hear you now, your rich voice deep and kind,
Rescuing a poem from time, bringing to mind
Lost centuries with a summoning word,
Lavishing on us who need much more of
What you gave, glimpses of heroic vision.

So you were angry at the pulling down
Of what recalled a finer age; you tried
To show how certain things destroyed, ignored,
Neglected was a crime against the past,
Impoverished the present. Some midland town
Attracted you, you stood in the waste
Places of an old church and, profoundly stirred,
Pondered how you could save what time had sorely tried,

Or else you cried in rage against the force
That would reduce to barren silence all
Who would articulate dark Ireland's soul;
You knew the evil of the pious curse,
The hearts that make God pitifully small
Until He seems the God of little fear
And not the God that you desired at all;
And yet you had the heart to do and dare.

I see you standing at your window,
Lifting a glass, watching the dying light
Along the quiet canal bank come and go
Until the time has come to say good-night:
You see me to the door; you lift a hand
Half-shyly, awkwardly, while I remark
Your soul's fine courtesy, my friend, and
Walk outside, alone, suddenly in the dark.

But in the dark or no, I realise
Your life's transcendent dignity,
A thing more wonderful than April skies
Emerging in compelling majesty,
Leaving mad March behind and making bloom
Each flower outstripping every weed and thorn;
Life rises from the crowded clay of doom,
Light dying promises the light reborn.

CHARLES J. KICKHAM (1830–1882)

My Ulick

My Ulick is sturdy and strong,
  And light is his foot on the heather,
And truth has been wed to his tongue
  Since first we were talking together.
And though he is lord of no lands,
  Nor castle, nor cattle, nor dairy,
My Ulick has health and his hands,
  And a heart-load of love for his Mary, —
    And what could a maiden wish more?

One night at the heel of the eve, —
  I mind it was snowing and blowing, —
My mother was knitting, I b'leeve,
  For me I was sitting and sewing;
My father had read o'er the news,
  And sat there a humming, "We'll wake him,"
When Ulick stepped in at the door,
  As white as the weather could make him: —
    True love never cooled with the frost.

He shook the snow out from his frieze,
  And drew a chair up to my father,
My heart lifted up to my eyes
  To see the two sitting together;
They talked of our isle and her wrongs
  Till both were as mad as starvation:
Then Ulick sang three or four songs,
  And closed with "Hurra for the Nation!" —
    O, Ulick, an Irishman still!

My father took him by the hand,
  Their hearts melted into each other;
While tears that she could not command
  Broke loose from the eyes of my mother.
"Ah, Freedom!" she cried, "wirra sthrue,
  A woman can say little in it;
But were it to come by you two,
  I've a guess at the way you would win it, —
    It would not be by weeping, I swear."

THOMAS KINSELLA (1928–   )

Thirty-three Triads
  Translated from the Irish (9th century)

THREE excellent qualities in narration:
  a good flow, depth of thought, conciseness.

THREE dislikeable qualities in the same:
  stiffness, obscurity, bad delivery.

THREE accomplishments well regarded in Ireland:
  a clever verse, music on the harp, the art of shaving
  faces.

THREE qualities that foster dignity:
  a handsome figure, fine memories, morality.

THREE things that foster high spirits:
  self-esteem, courting, drunkenness.

THREE things that are always ready in a decent man's
house:
beer, a bath, a good fire.

THREE uncomfortable welcomes:
a house busy with handicrafts, scalding water over
your feet, salty food and no drink to follow.

THREE things always ready in a bad house:
strife to confuse you, grousing, an ill-tempered hound.

THREE smiles that are worse than griefs:
the smile of snow melting, the smile of your wife when
another man has been with her, the smile of a mastiff
about to spring.

THREE darknesses into which it is not right for women
to go:
the darkness of mist, the darkness of the night, the
darkness of a wood.

THE THREE deafnesses of this world:
a doomed man faced with a warning, a beggar being
pitied, a headstrong woman hindered in lust.

THREE signs of concupiscence:
sighing, gamey tricks, going to hooleys.

THE THREE rudenesses of this world:
youth mocking at age, health mocking at sickness, a
wise man mocking a fool.

THREE times when silence is better than speech:
during instruction, during music, during preaching.

THREE times when speech is better than silence:

when urging a king to battle, when reciting a well
turned line of poetry, when giving due praise.

THREE sounds of increase:
the lowing of a cow in milk, the din of a smithy, the hiss
of the plough.

THE THREE places where the world is made new:
woman's womb, cow's udder, smith's anvil.

THREE ornaments of wisdom:
a large stock of facts, plenty of precedents, the use of a
good attorney.

THE THREE doors by which falsehood enters:
anger in stating the case, shaky information, evidence
from a bad memory.

THREE signs of thick-headedness:
long visits, staring, questioning without end.

THREE who throw their freedom away:
a lord who sells his land, a queen who takes up with a
boor, a poet's son who deserts the craft.

THREE signs of a rogue:
interrupting during a story, viciousness in play, telling
nasty jokes.

THE THREE boasts of a scoundrel:
I am after you like a shadow, I have trampled you
down, I have wet you with my clothes.

THREE excellent qualities in dress:
style, comfort, durability.

THE THREE signs of a dandy:
   the track of a comb in his hair, the trace of his bite in
   bread, the trail of a walking-stick behind him.

THE THREE with the lightest hearts:
   a student after reading his psalms, a young lad who
   has left off his boy's clothes for good, a maid who has
   been made a woman.

THREE slendernesses that best hold up the world:
   the jet of milk into the pail, the green blade of corn in
   the soil, the thread spinning out of a decent woman's
   fist.

THREE sicknesses that are better than good health:
   the pains of a woman bearing a son, a hot sickness in
   the bowels that will clean them out, a fever that purges
   evil.

THREE things required of a surgeon:
   a total cure, no scars, probing without pain.

THREE seething coldnesses:
   a well, the sea, new beer.

THREE coffers whose depths are shrouded in mystery:
   that of a prince, that of the Church, that of a well pa-
   tronised poet.

THREE scarcities that are better than abundance:
   a scarcity of fancy talk, a scarcity of cows in a small
   pasture, a scarcity of friends around the beer.

THREE things sacred to the men of Ireland:
   breast, knee, cheek.

FRANCIS LEDWIDGE (1891–1917)

The Wife of Llew

And Gwydion said to Math, when it was Spring:
"Come now and let us make a wife for Llew."
And so they broke broad boughs yet moist with dew,
And in a shadow made a magic ring:
They took the violet and the meadow-sweet
To form her pretty face, and for her feet
They built a mound of daisies on a wing,
And for her voice they made a linnet sing
In the wide poppy blowing for her mouth.
And over all they chanted twenty hours.
And Llew came singing from the azure south
And bore away his wife of birds and flowers.

Had I a Golden Pound
(*After the Irish*)

Had I a golden pound to spend,
My love should mend and sew no more.
And I would buy her a little quern,
Easy to turn on the kitchen floor.

And for her windows curtains white,
With birds in flight and flowers in bloom,
To face with pride the road to town,
And mellow down her sunlit room.

And with the silver change we'd prove
The truth of Love to life's own end,
With hearts the years could but embolden,
Had I a golden pound to spend.

SHANE LESLIE (1885–1971)

Prayer for Fine Weather

Saint Joseph, Saint Peter, Saint Paul!
Encounter the rain that it stops:
Saint Patrick, whatever befall
Keep an eye on the state of the crops!

Saint Andrew, Saint John, and Saint James,
Preserve us from deluge and floods:
If the Fiend takes to watery games,
Have pity at least on the spuds.

Muckish Mountain (*The Pig's Back*)

Like a sleeping swine upon the skyline,
Muckish, thou art shadowed out,
Grubbing up the rubble of the ages
With your broken, granite snout.

Muckish, greatest pig in Ulster's oakwoods,
Littered out of rock and fire,
Deep you thrust your mottled flanks for cooling
Underneath the peaty mire.

Long before the Gael was young in Ireland,
You were ribbed and old and grey,
Muckish, you have long outstayed his staying,
You have seen him swept away.

Muckish, you will not forget the people
Of the laughing speech and eye,
They who gave you name of Pig-back-mountain
And the Heavens for a sty!

WINIFRID M. LETTS (1882–   )

Fantasia

"I love my love with an M," said I,
He's merry, masterful, mad.
He bade me dress and come out to dine
On the last gold piece he had.
"We'll feast tonight at the Old Moor's Head,
The tavern with creaking sign, then tread
A Morris dance with a motley crew
Till hooves and slippers are wet with dew."

"What is your taste?" quoth he to me,
"A golden beaker of Malvoisie?
Mushrooms picked by a Harvest moon,
Served with a silver platter and spoon?
Ice-cold melon and marzipan?"

Monkeys, solemn in livery,
Served at a table, one, two, three.
"Monkeys! Flunkeys! quick as you can
Fetch me mead in a pewter jug,
Pretty one here shall kiss the mug,
Mince-pies served on a copper pan,
And bring the score for the night is late."
A gold moidore he threw on the plate.

Danced we up and danced we down
Till the moon turned pale with a peevish frown,
And someone was knocking with knock-tock-tock,
And six chimes rang on the kitchen clock.
"Daughter! daughter! why do you drowse?
Over the barn I see the sun,
The wren is singing, the day begun.
Get up you slut and go milk the cows."

WINIFRID M. LETTS

The Bold Unbiddable Child

Now what is he after below in the street?
  (God save us, he's terrible wild!)
Is it stirrin' the gutter around with his feet?
He'd best be aware when the two of us meet.
        Come in out o' that,
        Come in,
        You bold unbiddable child!

He's after upsetting the Widow Foy's pail —
  She'll murder him yet, Widow Foy!
An' he's pulling the massacree dog by the tail,
By the hokey! that young one is born for the jail.
        Come in out o' that,
        Come in,
        You rogue of a villyainous boy!

Go tell him his mother is seeking a stick
  For a boy that is terrible wild.
If he cares for his feelings he'd better be quick,
Och! he'll draw in his horns when he sees me, will Mick.
      Come in out o' that,
      Come in,
      You bold unbiddable child!

The Choice

Saint Joseph, let you send me a comrade true and kind,
For the one I'm after seeking, it beats the world to find.

There's Christy Shee's a decent lad, but he's too lank and
    tall;
And Shaneen Burke will never do, for he's a foot too
    small.

John Heffernan has gold enough, but sure he'd have me
    bet
With talkin' of the wife that died a year before we met.

Young Pat Delaney suits my mind, but he's a thrifle wild;
And Tim I've known too well itself from since I was a
    child.

Old Dennis Morrissey has pigs, and cattle in the byre,
But, someways, I don't fancy him the far side o' the fire.

I'd have Saint Joseph choose me a comrade rich and
    kind —
And if it's Terry Sullivan — maybe I mightn't mind.

CHARLES LEVER (1806–1872)

It's Little for Glory I Care

It's little for glory I care;
  Sure ambition is only a fable;
I'd as soon be myself as Lord Mayor,
  With lashins of drink on the table.
I like to lie down in the sun,
  And drame when my faytures is scorchin',
That when I'm too ould for more fun,
  Why, I'll marry a wife with a fortune.

And in winter, with bacon and eggs,
  And a place at the turf-fire basking,
Sip my punch as I roasted my legs,
  Oh! the devil a more I'd be asking.
For I haven't a jaynius for work, —
  It was never the gift of the Bradies, —
But I'd make a most illigant Turk,
  For I'm fond of tobacco and ladies.

The Pope He Leads a Happy Life

The Pope he leads a happy life,
He knows no cares nor marriage strife;
He drinks the best of Rhenish wine —
I would the Pope's gay lot were mine.

But yet not happy is his life —
He loves no maid or wedded wife,
Nor child has he to cheer his hope —
I would not wish to be the Pope.

The Sultan better pleases me,
He leads a life of jollity,
Has wives as many as he will —
I would the Sultan's throne then fill.

But yet he's not a happy man —
He must obey the Alcoran:
He dare not drink one drop of wine —
I would not change his lot for mine.

So here I'll take my lowly stand,
I'll drink my own, my native land;
I'll kiss my maiden fair and fine,
And drink the best of Rhenish wine.

And when my maiden kisses me,
I'll think that I the Sultan be;
And when my Rhenish wine I tope,
I'll fancy then I am the Pope.

SAMUEL LOVER (1797–1868)

Paddy O'Rafther

Paddy, in want of a dinner one day,
Credit all gone, and no money to pay,
Stole from a priest a fat pullet, they say,
    And went to confession just afther;
"Your riv'rince," says Paddy, "I stole this fat hen."
"What, what!" says the priest. "At your ould thricks again?
Faith, you'd rather be staalin' than sayin' *amen,*
                        Paddy O'Rafther!"

"Sure, you wouldn't be angry," says Pat, "if you knew
That the best of intintions I had in my view—
For I stole it to make it a present to you,
   And you can absolve me afther."
"Do you think," says the priest, "I'd partake of your theft?
Of your seven small senses you must be bereft—
You're the biggest blackguard that I know, right and left,
                  Paddy O'Rafther."

"Then what shall I do with the pullet," says Pat,
"If your riv'rince won't take it? By this and by that
I don't know no more than a dog or a cat
   What your riv'rince would have me be afther."
"Why, then," says his rev'rence, "you sin-blinded owl,
Give back to the man that you stole from his fowl:
For if you do not, 'twill be worse for your sowl,
                  Paddy O'Rafther."

Says Paddy, "I ask'd him to take it—'tis thrue
As this minit I'm talkin', your riv'rince, to you;
But he wouldn't resaive it—so what can I do?"
   Says Paddy, nigh choken with laughter.
"By my throth," says the priest, "but the case is absthruse;
If he won't take his hen, why the man is a goose:
'Tis not the first time my advice was no use,
                  Paddy O'Rafther."

"But, for sake of your sowl, I would sthrongly advise
To someone in want you would give your supplies—
Some widow, or orphan, with tears in their eyes;
   And *then* you may come to *me* afther."
So Paddy went off to the brisk Widow Hoy,
And the pullet between them was eaten with joy,
And, says she, "'Pon my word you're the cleverest boy,
                  Paddy O'Rafther."

Then Paddy went back to the priest the next day,
And told him the fowl he had given away
To a poor lonely widow, in want and dismay,
   The loss of her spouse weeping afther.
"Well, now," says the priest, "I'll absolve you, my lad,
For repentantly making the best of the bad,
In feeding the hungry and cheering the sad,
                   Paddy O'Rafther!"

Lanty Leary

Bold Lanty was in love, you see, with lively Rosie Carey,
But her father wouldn't give the girl to slippery Lanty
    Leary;
   Come on for fun, says she, we'll run,
   My father's so contrairy,
Won't you follow me where'er I be? I will, says Lanty
    Leary.

One day her father died on her, and not from drinking
    water,
House, land, and cash he left, they say, by will to Rose
    his daughter,
   Come on for fun, says she, we'll run
   To a place more bright and airy,
Won't you follow me where'er I be? More than ever now,
    says Leary.

But Rose herself was taken ill and each day worse was
    growing,
And Lanty dear, says she, I fear into my grave I'm going;
   You can't survive, says she, nor thrive
   Without your Rosie Carey
Won't you follow me where'er I be? I'll not, says Lanty
    Leary.

DONAGH MacDONAGH (1912–1968)

Dublin Made Me

Dublin made me and no little town
With the country closing in on its streets,
The cattle walking proudly on its pavements,
The jobbers, the gombeenmen and the cheats

Devouring the Fair Day between them,
A public-house to half a hundred men,
And the teacher, the solicitor and the bank-clerk
In the hotel bar, drinking for ten.

Dublin made me, not the secret poteen still,
The raw and hungry hills of the West,
The lean road flung over profitless bog
Where only a snipe could nest,

Where the sea takes its tithe of every boat.
Bawneen and curragh have no allegiance of mine,
Nor the cute, self-deceiving talkers of the South
Who look to the East for a sign.

The soft and dreary midlands with their tame canals
Wallow between sea and sea, remote from adventure,
And Northward a far and fortified province
Crouches under the lash of arid censure.

I disclaim all fertile meadows, all tilled land,
The evil that grows from it, and the good,
But the Dublin of old statutes, this arrogant city,
Stirs proudly and secretly in my blood.

A Revel

I'd fill up the house with guests this minute
And have them drinking in every room
And the laughter wrecking the garden quiet.
Citymen dressed in a sober style
Who never soiled a buckled shoe,
And wild country boys with a frieze coat flapping
That were never within an ass's roar
Of a city street, and shining girls
In every fashion. I'd call them in
Out of every year for the past ten hundred
And make them safe at their own table,
The men whose blood is safe in my veins.

I'd have no aged ghosts struggling out of the grave,
But lively lads that I'd borrow from time,
And till Peter's bird set them screaming homeward
The neighbours hearing that heady laughter
Would think it a wedding or a wake.

I'd leave uncertain the hour of departure,
But while night was pasted black on the windows
We'd talk of love, and blood to blood
We'd speak one language; tinker and poet,
The tramps who were hurled from their own possessions
And the wealthy men would talk flesh to flesh,
The years dissolved that were huge between them.

And one would tell of the time of hunger,
The mouths stained green in a ditch's end,
Earth cleared for action and hunger rearing
High in the belly, a country withered
Before Spring's rally. But another would shout

Of a night of drinking, the senses loosed
And the traces broken
And the drink as mild as the milky way.

Fathers would lean on their grandsons' shoulders
And great-great-grandsons pass a glass
And laugh in the face of their great-grandfather;
And together we'd find the spirit within us
Too wild to be bound by house or wall,
And only the dawn and the cock's alarm
Could save the town. Then home they'd rush
Hot in their leather.

Heir to them all
I'd count them over, recall the nose
And the curve of the mouth, till sleep would slip
Through the wakening window and curl about me,
And I, like them, would be lost in time.

THOMAS MacDONAGH (1878–1916)

The Night Hunt

In the morning, in the dark,
When the stars begin to blunt,
By the wall of Barna Park
Dogs I heard and saw them hunt.
All the parish dogs were there,
All the dogs for miles around,
Teeming up behind a hare,
In the dark, without a sound.

How I heard I scarce can tell —
'Twas a patter in the grass —
And I did not see them well
Come across the dark and pass;
Yet I saw them and I knew
Spearman's dog and Spellman's dog
And, beside my own dog too,
Leamy's from the Island Bog.

In the morning when the sun
Burnished all the green to gorse,
I went out to take a run
Round the bog upon my horse;
And my dog that had been sleeping
In the heat beside the door
Left his yawning and went leaping
On a hundred yards before.

Through the village street we passed —
Not a dog there raised a snout —
Through the street and out at last
On the white bog road and out
Over Barna Park full pace,
Over to the Silver Stream,
Horse and dog in happy race,
Rider between thought and dream.

By the stream at Leamy's house,
Lay a dog — my pace I curbed —
But our coming did not rouse
Him from drowsing undisturbed;
And my dog, as unaware
Of the other, dropped beside
And went running by me there
With my horse's slackened stride.

Yet by something, by a twitch
Of the sleeper's eye, a look
From the runner, something which
Little chords of feeling shook,
I was conscious that a thought
Shuddered through the silent deep
Of a secret — I had caught
Something I had known in sleep.

John-John

I dreamt last night of you, John-John,
    And thought you called to me;
And when I woke this morning, John,
    Yourself I hoped to see;
But I was all alone, John-John,
    Though still I heard your call;
I put my boots and bonnet on,
    And took my Sunday shawl,
And went, full sure to find you, John,
        At Nenagh fair.

The fair was just the same as then,
    Five years ago today,
When first you left the thimble men
    And came with me away;
For there again were thimble men
    And shooting galleries,
And card trick men and Maggie-men
    Of all sorts and degrees;
But not a sight of you, John-John,
        Was anywhere.

I turned my face to home again,
    And called myself a fool
To think you'd leave the thimble men
    And live again by rule,
And go to mass and keep the fast
    And till the little patch;
My wish to have you home was past
    Before I raised the latch
And pushed the door and saw you, John,
        Sitting down there.

How cool you came in here, begad,
   As if you owned the place!
But rest yourself there now, my lad,
   'Tis good to see your face;
My dream is out, and now by it
   I think I know my mind:
At six o'clock this house you'll quit,
   And leave no grief behind; —
But until six o'clock, John-John,
       My bit you'll share.

The neighbours' shame of me began
   When first I brought you in;
To wed and keep a tinker man
   They thought a kind of sin;
But now this three year since you're gone
   'Tis pity me they do,
And that I'd rather have, John-John,
   Than that they'd pity you,
Pity for me and you, John-John,
       I could not bear.

Oh, you're my husband right enough,
   But what's the good of that?
You know you never were the stuff
   To be the cottage cat,
To watch the fire and hear me lock
   The door and put out Shep —
But there, now, it is six o'clock
   And time for you to step.
God bless and keep you far, John-John!
       And that's my prayer.

PATRICK MacDONOGH (1902–1961)

Dodona's Oaks Were Still

He told the barmaid he had things to do,
Such as to find out what we are and why.
He said, I must have winter in the mountains;
Spring is no good, nor summer,
And even autumn carries too much colour.
I must have winter. Winter's naked line
Is truth revealed and there's a discipline
Along the edges of gaunt rocks on frosty nights.

She said she thought so too,
And so he left
Bookshops and music and the sight of friends,
Good smokeroom laughter starred with epigrams,
Seven sweet bridges and those bucking trams
That blunder west through bitter history, —
And women,
Perhaps particularly women,
Climbing like slow white maggots through his thought;
He left the lot,
And got him to a shack above the city,
Lit a white candle to his solitude
And searched among the images he'd seen
Of his own self in other minds to find
Mankind in him.
He hoped to see the whole
Diverse and complicated world
Fold up and pack itself into his soul
The way a walnut's packed.
The lonely fool,
Squatting among the heavy mountain shapes,
Looked on the wet black branches and the red,
Followed the urgent branches to their tips
And back again through twig and stem to root,
Always alone and busy with himself,
Enquiring if this world of decent men
Must be hell's kitchen to the end of time,
Because of that old sin, intolerable pride,
Strong powers of angels soured by impotence,
Rebellious godhead working its hot way
Through tangled veins.
He cried in pain towards the writhing trees,
But heard no voice.
Dodona's oaks were still.

She Walked Unaware

O, she walked unaware of her own increasing beauty
That was holding men's thoughts from market
      or plough,
As she passed by, intent on her womanly duties,
And she without leisure to be wayward or proud;
Or if she had pride then it was not in her thinking
But thoughtless in her body like a flower of good
      breeding.
The first time I saw her spreading coloured linen
Beyond the green willow she gave me gentle greeting
With no more intention than the leaning willow tree.

Though she smiled without intention yet from that
      day forward
Her beauty filled like water the four corners of my
      being,
And she rested in my heart like the hare in the form
That is shaped to herself. And I that would be singing
Or whistling at all times went silently then;
Till I drew her aside among straight stems of beeches
When the blackbird was sleeping and promised
      that never
The fields would be ripe but I'd gather all sweetness,
A red moon of August would rise on our wedding.

October is spreading bright flame along stripped willows
Low fires of the dogwood burn down to grey water, —
God pity me now and all desolate sinners
Demented with beauty! I have blackened my thought
In drouths of bad longing, and all brightness goes
      shrouded
Since he came with his rapture of wild words that
      mirrored
Her beauty and made her ungentle and proud.
Tonight she will spread her brown hair on his pillow
But I shall be hearing the harsh cries of wild fowl.

Song

She spoke to me gently with words of sweet meaning,
    Like the damsel was leaning on Heaven's
        half-door,
And her bright eyes besought me to leave off deceiving
    And trouble the parish with scandal no more.

And there, for a moment, I thought I'd be better
    To take those round arms for a halter and live
Secure and respectable, safe in her shelter,
    And be the bright pattern of boys in the village.

But I thought how the lane would have sheltering
        shadows
    And a glass on the counter would look as before;
And the house was too dark, and her eyes were too
        narrow,
    So I left her alone at her door.

The Widow of Drynam

I stand in my door and look over the low field of Dry-
    nam.
No man but the one man has known me, no child but
    the one

Grew big at my breast, and what are my sorrows beside
That pride and that glory? I come from devotions on
    Sunday
And leave them to pity or spite; and though I who had
    music have none
But crying of seagulls at morning and calling of curlews
    at night,
I wake and remember my beauty and think of my son
Who would stare the loud fools into silence
And rip the dull parish asunder.

Small wonder indeed he was wild with breeding and
    beauty
And why would my proud lad not straighten his back
    from the plough?
My son was not got and I bound in a cold bed of duty
Nor led to the side of the road by some clay-clabbered
    lout!
No, but rapt by a passionate poet away from the dancers
To curtains and silver and firelight, —
O wisely and gently he drew down the pale shell of satin
And all the bright evening's adornment and clad me
Again in the garment of glory, the joy of his eyes.

I stand in my door and look over the low fields of Dry-
    nam
When skies move westward, the way he will come from
    the war;
Maybe on a morning of March when a thin sun is shining
And starlings have blackened the thorn,
He will come, my bright limb of glory, my mettlesome
    wild one,
With coin in his pocket and tales on the tip of his tongue,
And the proud ones that slight me will bring back for-
    gotten politeness
To see me abroad on the roads with my son,
The two of us laughing together or stepping in silence.

111

MÁIRE MacENTEE (1922–   )

Irish Curse on the Occupying English
Translated from the Irish (20th century)

May we never taste of death nor quit this vale of tears
Until we see the Englishry go begging down the years,
Packs on their backs to earn a penny pay,
In little leaking boots, as we did in our day.

SEUMAS MacMANUS (1869–1960)

A Health to the Birds

Here's a health to the birds one and all!
A health to the birds great and small!
The birds that from hill and hedge call,
Through the highlands and islands of grey Donegal —
Here's a health to them,
*   Health to them,*
*   Health to them all!*

Here's a health to the mavis!
A health to the mavis that sits on the thorn,
And trolls a gay breastful to brighten the morn,
And lighten the load of the man in the corn!
May its breast ne'er be tuneless its heart ne'er forlorn —
      A health to the mavis!

Here's a health to the leverock!
A health to the leverock that loves the blue sky!
No bog is too low, no hill is too high,
And the moor's not too poor, for the leverock to lie:
May its name, and its fame, and its song, never die!
      A health to the leverock!

Here's a health to the linnet!
A health to the linnet that lilts on the tree,
The little green linnet so pretty to see,
The linnet whose tinkling tones gladden the lea—
High health, and heart-wealth, little linnet, to thee!
A health to the linnet!

Here's a health to the blackbird!
A health to the blackbird who hides in the bush,
In the glen, far from men, where the dark rivers rush,
And rolls a full soul in the round notes that gush
From his silver-toned throat at dawning's first flush—
A health to the blackbird!

Here's a health to the wren!
Ay, a health to the wren, too, the devil's dear pet,
Though thousands of years he's owed a black debt,
And it's often we've made the vile thummikin sweat—
But, away with old scores! forgive and forget!
Here's a health to the wren!

Here's a health to the birds one and all!
A health to the birds great and small—
The birds that from hill and hedge call,
Through the highlands and islands of grey Donegal—
Here's a health to them,
Health to them,
Health to them all!

[AUTHOR'S NOTE: It was a wren, we say, that betrayed to the soldiers the whereabouts of our Saviour: so, our lads persecute it.]

LOUIS MacNEICE (1907–1963)

Glass Falling

The glass is going down. The sun
Is going down. The forecasts say
It will be warm, with frequent showers.
We ramble down the showery hours
And amble up and down the day.
Mary will wear her black goloshes
And splash the puddles on the town;
And soon on fleets of macintoshes
The rain is coming down, the frown
Is coming down of heaven showing
A wet night coming, the glass is going
Down, the sun is going down.

Dublin

Grey brick upon brick
Declamatory bronze
On somber pedestals —
O'Connell, Grattan, Moore —
And the brewery tugs and the swans
On the balustraded stream
And the bare bones of a fanlight
Over a hungry door
And the air soft on the cheek
And porter running from the taps
With a head of yellow cream
And Nelson on his pillar
Watching his world collapse.

This was never my town,
I was not born nor bred
Nor schooled here and she will not

Have me alive or dead
But yet she holds my mind
With her seedy elegance,
With her gentle veils of rain
And all her ghosts that walk
And all that hide behind
Her Regency façades —
The catcalls and the pain,
The glamour of her squalor
The bravado of her talk.

The lights jig in the river
With a concertina movement,
And the sun comes up in the morning
Like barley-sugar on the water,
And the mist on the Wicklow hills
Is close, as close
As the peasantry were to the landlord,
As the Irish to the Anglo-Irish,
As the killer is close one moment
To the man he kills,
Or as the moment itself
Is close to the next moment.

She is not an Irish town
And she is not English,
Historic with guns and vermin
And the cold renown
Of a fragment of Church Latin,
Of an oratorical phrase.
But O the days are soft,
Soft enough to forget
The lessons better learnt,
The bullet on the wet

Streets, the crooked deal,
The steel behind the laugh,
The Four Courts burnt.

Fort of the Dane,
Garrison of the Saxon,
Augustan capitol
Of a Gaelic nation,
Appropriating all
The alien brought,
You give me time for thought
And by a juggler's trick
You poise the toppling hour —
O greyness run to flower,
Grey stone, grey water,
And brick upon grey brick.

Prayer Before Birth

I am not yet born; O hear me.
Let not the bloodsucking bat or the rat or the stoat or the
        club-footed ghoul come near me.

I am not yet born; console me.
I fear that the human race may with tall walls wall me,
        with strong drugs dope me, with wise lies lure me,
        on black racks rack me, in blood-baths roll me.

I am not yet born; provide me
With water to dandle me, grass to grow for me, trees to
        talk to me, sky to sing to me, birds and a white light
        in the back of my mind to guide me.

I am not yet born; forgive me
For the sins that in me the world shall commit, my words
    when they speak me, my thoughts when they think
    me, my treason engendered by traitors beyond
    me, my life when they murder by means of my
    hands, my death when they live me.

I am not yet born; rehearse me
In the parts I must play and the cues I must take when
    old men lecture me, bureaucrats hector me, moun-
    tains frown on me, lovers laugh at me, the white
    waves call me to folly and the desert calls
    me to doom and the beggar refuses
    my gift and my children curse me.

I am not yet born; O hear me,
Let not the man who is beast or who thinks he is God
    come near me.

I am not yet born; O fill me
With strength against those who would freeze my
    humanity, would dragoon me into a lethal automaton,
    would make me a cog in a machine, a thing with
    one face, a thing, and against all those
    who would dissipate my entirety, would
    blow me like thistledown hither and
    thither or hither and thither
    like water held in the
    hands would spill me.
Let them not make me a stone and let them not spill me.
Otherwise kill me.

DEREK MAHON (1941–   )

The Prisoner

For several days I have been under
House-arrest. My table has become
A sundial to its empty bottle.
With wise abandon
Lover and friend have gone.

In the window opposite
An old lady sits each afternoon
Talking to no one. I shout.
Either she is deaf or
She has reason.

I have books, provisions, running water
And a little stove. It would not matter
If cars moved silently at night
And no light or laughter
Came from the houses down the street.

It is taking longer than almost anything —
But I know, when it is over
And back come friend and lover,
I shall forget it like a childhood illness
Or a sleepless night-crossing.

Exit Molloy

Now at the end I smell the smells of spring
Where in a dark ditch I lie wintering —
And the little town only a mile away,
Happy and fatuous in the light of day.
A bell tolls gently. I should start to cry
But my eyes are closed and my face dry.
I am not important and I have to die.
Strictly speaking, I am already dead,
But still I can hear the birds sing on over my head.

FRANCIS S. MAHONY (FATHER PROUT)
(1804–1866)

The Piper's Progress

When I was a boy
In my father's mud edifice,
Tender and bare
    As a pig in a sty:
Out of the door as I
Look'd with a steady phiz,
Who but Thade Murphy
    The piper went by.
Says Thady, "But few play
This music — can you play?"
Says I, "I can't tell,
    For I never did try."
So he told me that *he* had a charm
    To make the pipes purtily speak;
Then squeezed a bag under his arm,
    When sweetly they set up a squeak!

Fa-ra-la-la-ra-la-loo!
Och hone!
How he handled the drone!
And then the sweet music he blew
Would have melted the heart of a
stone!

"Your pipe," says I, "Thady,
So neatly comes o'er me,
Naked I'll wander
Wherever it blows:
And if my poor parents
Should try to recover me,
Sure, it won't be
By describing my clothes.
The music I hear now
Takes hold of my ear now,

And leads me all over
 The world by the nose."
So I follow'd his bagpipe so sweet,
 And I sung as I leap'd like a frog,
"Adieu to my family seat,
 So pleasantly placed in a bog."
  Fa-ra-la-la-ra-la-loo!
   Och hone!
  How we handled the drone!
And then the sweet music we blew
 Would have melted the heart of
  a stone!

Full five years I follow'd him,
Nothing could sunder us;
Till he one morning
 Had taken a sup,
And slipt from a bridge
In a river just under us
Souse to the bottom
 Just like a blind pup.
He roar'd and he bawl'd out;
And I also call'd out,
"Now Thady, my friend,
 Don't you mean to come up?"
He was dead as a nail in a door —
 Poor Thady was laid on the shelf.
So I took up his pipes on the shore,
 And now I've set up for myself.
  Fa-ra-la-la-ra-la-loo!
   Och hone!
  Don't I handle the drone!
And play such sweet music? I, too,
 Can't I soften the heart of a
  stone!

FRANCIS S. MAHONY (FATHER PROUT)

The Shandon Bells

Sabbata pango
Funera plango
Solemnia clango

Inscription on an old bell.

With deep affection
And recollection
I often think of
    Those Shandon bells,
Whose sounds so wild would,
In the days of childhood,
Fling round my cradle
    Their magic spells.
On this I ponder
Where'er I wander,
And thus grow fonder,
    Sweet Cork, of thee,
With thy bells of Shandon,
That sound so grand on
The pleasant waters
    Of the river Lee.

I've heard bells chiming
Full many a clime in,
Tolling sublime in
    Cathedral shrine,
While at a glib rate
Brass tongues would vibrate —
But all their music
    Spoke naught like thine;
For memory dwelling
On each proud swelling
Of the belfry knelling

Its bold notes free,
Made the bells of Shandon
Sound far more grand on
The pleasant waters
  Of the river Lee.

I've heard bells tolling
Old "Adrian's Mole" in
Their thunder rolling
  From the Vatican,
And cymbals glorious
Swinging uproarious
In the gorgeous turrets
  Of Notre Dame;
But thy sounds were sweeter
Than the dome of Peter
Flings o'er the Tiber
  Pealing solemnly;—
Oh! the bells of Shandon
Sound far more grand on
The pleasant waters
  Of the river Lee.

There's a bell in Moscow,
While a tower and kiosk o!
In Saint Sophia
  The Turkman gets,
And loud in air
Calls men to prayer
From the tapering summit
  Of tall minarets.
Such empty phantom
I freely grant them;
But there is an anthem

More dear to me, —
'Tis the bells of Shandon
That sound so grand on
The pleasant waters
Of the river Lee.

JAMES CLARENCE MANGAN (1803–1849)

Shapes and Signs

I see black dragons mount the sky,
  I see earth yawn beneath my feet —
    I feel within the asp, the worm
That will not sleep and cannot die,
  Fair though may show the winding-sheet!
    I hear all night as through a storm
    Hoarse voices calling, calling
      My name upon the wind —
    All omens monstrous and appalling
      Affright my guilty mind.

I exult alone in one wild hour —
  That hour in which the red cup drowns
    The memories it anon renews
In ghastlier guise, in fiercer power —
  Then Fancy brings me golden crowns,
    And visions of all brilliant hues
    Lap my lost soul in gladness,
      Until I wake again,
    And the dark lava-fires of madness
      Once more sweep through my brain.

The Woman of Three Cows
Translated from the Irish

> O woman of Three Cows, *agra!* don't let your tongue thus
>   rattle!
> Oh, don't be saucy, don't be stiff, because you may have
>   cattle.
> I have seen — and, here's my hand to you, I only say what's
>   true —
> A many a one with twice your stock not half so proud as
>   you.
>
> Good luck to you, don't scorn the poor, and don't be their
>   despiser;
> For worldly wealth soon melts away, and cheats the very
>   miser;

And Death soon strips the proudest wreath from haughty
    human brows —
Then don't be stiff, and don't be proud, good Woman of
    Three Cows!

See where Momonia's heroes lie, proud Owen Mór's de-
    scendants,
'Tis they that won the glorious name, and had the grand
    attendants;
If *they* were forced to bow to Fate, as every mortal bows,
Can *you* be proud, can *you* be stiff, my Woman of Three
    Cows?

The brave sons of the Lord of Clare, they left the land to
    mourning;
Mavrone! for they were banished, with no hope of their
    returning.
Who knows in what abodes of want those youths were
    driven to house?
Yet *you* can give yourself these airs, O Woman of Three
    Cows.

O, think of Donnell of the Ships, the Chief whom nothing
    daunted,
See how he fell in distant Spain unchronicled, unchanted!
He sleeps, the great O'Sullivan, where thunder cannot
    rouse —
Then ask yourself, should *you* be proud, good Woman of
    Three Cows?

O'Ruark, Maguire, those souls of fire, whose names are
    shrined in story:
Think how their high achievements once made Erin's
    greatest glory.

Yet now their bones lie mouldering under weeds and
    cypress boughs —
And so, for all your pride, will yours, O Woman of Three
    Cows.

Th' O'Carrolls, also, famed when fame was only for the
    boldest,
Rest in forgotten sepulchres with Erin's best and oldest;
Yet who so great as they of yore in battle or carouse?
Just think of that, and hide your head, good Woman of
    Three Cows.

Your neighbour's poor; and you, it seems, are big with
    vain ideas,
Because, forsooth, you've got three cows — one more, I
    see, than *she* has;
That tongue of yours wags more at times than charity
    allows;
But if you're strong, be merciful — great Woman of Three
    Cows.

Avran:
Now, there you go; you still, of course, keep up your
    scornful bearing,
And I'm too poor to hinder you; but, by the cloak I'm
    wearing,
If I had but *four* cows myself, even though you were my
    spouse,
I'd thwack you well, to cure your pride, my Woman of
    Three Cows.

[*agra:* my love]
[*Mavrone:* my sorrow]
[*Avran:* summing up]

Dark Rosaleen
Translated from the Irish (probably 16th century)

O, my Dark Rosaleen,
   Do not sigh, do not weep!
The priests are on the ocean green,
   They march along the Deep.
There's wine from the royal Pope,
   Upon the ocean green;
And Spanish ale shall give you hope,
   My Dark Rosaleen!
   My own Rosaleen!
Shall glad your heart, shall give you hope,
Shall give you health, and help, and hope,
   My Dark Rosaleen!

Over hills, and through dales,
   Have I roamed for your sake;
All yesterday I sailed with sails
   On river and on lake.
The Erne, at its highest flood,
   I dashed across unseen,
For there was lightning in my blood,
   My Dark Rosaleen!
   My own Rosaleen!
Oh! there was lightning in my blood,
Red lightning lightened through my blood,
   My Dark Rosaleen!

All day long, in unrest,
   To and fro, do I move.
The very soul within my breast
   Is wasted for you, love!
The heart in my bosom faints

To think of you, my Queen,
My life of life, my saint of saints,
    My Dark Rosaleen!
    My own Rosaleen!
To hear your sweet and sad complaints,
My life, my love, my saint of saints,
    My Dark Rosaleen!

Woe and pain, pain and woe,
    Are my lot, night and noon,
To see your bright face clouded so,
    Like to the mournful moon.
But yet will I rear your throne
    Again in golden sheen;
'Tis you shall reign, shall reign alone,
    My Dark Rosaleen!
    My own Rosaleen!
'Tis you shall have the golden throne,
'Tis you shall reign, and reign alone,
    My Dark Rosaleen!

Over dews, over sands,
    Will I fly, for your weal:
Your holy, delicate white hands
    Shall girdle me with steel.
At home in your emerald bowers,
    From morning's dawn till e'en,
You'll pray for me, my flower of flowers,
    My Dark Rosaleen!
    My fond Rosaleen!
You'll think of me through daylight's hours,
My virgin flower, my flower of flowers,
    My Dark Rosaleen!

I could scale the blue air,
  I could plough the high hills,
Oh, I could kneel all night in prayer,
  To heal your many ills!
And one beamy smile from you
  Would float like light between
My toils and me, my own, my true,
  My Dark Rosaleen!
  My fond Rosaleen!
Would give me life and soul anew,
A second life, a soul anew,
  My Dark Rosaleen!

O! the Erne shall run red
  With redundance of blood,
The earth shall rock beneath our tread,
  And flames wrap hill and wood,
And gun-peal, and slogan cry
  Wake many a glen serene,
Ere you shall fade, ere you shall die,
  My Dark Rosaleen!
  My own Rosaleen!
The Judgment Hour must first be nigh,
Ere you can fade, ere you can die,
  My Dark Rosaleen!

KUNO MEYER (1859–1919)

The Fort of Rathangan
   Translated from the Irish

> The fort over against the oak-wood,
> Once it was Bruidge's, it was Cathal's,
> It was Aed's, it was Ailill's,
> It was Conaing's, it was Cuilíne's
> And it was Maeldúin's;
> The fort remains after each in his turn—
> And the king's asleep in the ground.

A Song of Winter
Translated from the Irish (10th century)

Cold, cold!
Cold to-night is broad Moylurg,
Higher the snow than the mountain range,
The deer cannot get at their food.

Cold till Doom!
The storm has spread over all:
A river is each furrow upon the slope,
Each ford a full pool.

A great tidal sea is each loch,
A full loch is each pool:
Horses cannot get over the ford of Ross,
No more can two feet get there.

The fish of Ireland are a-roaming,
There is no strand which the wave does not pound,
Not a town there is in the land,
Not a bell is heard, no crane talks.

The wolves of Cuan-wood get
Neither rest nor sleep in their lair,
The little wren cannot find
Shelter in her nest on the slope of Lon.

Keen wind and cold ice
Has burst upon the little company of birds,
The blackbird cannot get a lee to her liking,
Shelter for its side in Cuan-wood.

Cozy our pot on its hook,
Crazy the hut on the slope of Lon:
The snow has crushed the wood here,
Toilsome to climb up Ben-bo.

Glenn Rye's ancient bird
From the bitter wind gets grief;
Great her misery and her pain,
The ice will get into her mouth.

From flock and from down to rise—
Take it to heart!—were folly for thee:
Ice in heaps on every ford—
That is why I say "cold"!

Eve's Lament
Translated from the Irish (10th–11th century)

I am Eve, great Adam's wife,
'Tis I that outraged Jesus of old;
'Tis I that robbed my children of Heaven,
By rights 'tis I that should have gone upon the cross.

I had a kingly house to please me,
Grievous the evil choice that disgraced me,
Grievous the wicked advice that withered me!
Alas! my hand is not pure.

'Tis I that plucked the apple,
Which went across my gullet:
So long as they endure in the light of day,
So long women will not cease from folly.

There would be no ice in any place,
There would be no glistening windy winter,
There would be no hell, there would be no sorrow,
There would be no fear, if it were not for me.

From *The Vision of Mac Conglinne*
Translated from the Irish (12th century)

A vision that appeared to me,
An apparition wonderful
      I tell to all:
There was a coracle all of lard
Within a port of New-milk Lake
      Upon the world's smooth sea.

We went into that man-of-war,
'Twas warrior-like to take the road
      O'er ocean's heaving waves.
Our oar-strokes then we pulled
Across the level of the main,
Throwing the sea's harvest up
      Like honey, the sea-soil.

The fort we reached was beautiful,
With works of custards thick,
      Beyond the lake.
Fresh butter was the bridge in front,
The rubble dyke was fair white wheat,
      Bacon the palisade.

Stately, pleasantly it sat,
A compact house and strong.
    Then I went in:
The door of it was hung beef,
The threshold was dry bread,
    Cheese-curds the walls.

Smooth pillars of old cheese
And sappy bacon props
    Alternate ranged;
Stately beams of mellow cream,
White posts of real curds
    Kept up the house.

Behind it was a well of wine,
Beer and bragget in streams,
    Each full pool to the taste.
Malt in smooth wavy sea
Over a lard-spring's brink
    Flowed through the floor.

A lake of juicy pottage
Under a cream of oozy lard
    Lay 'twixt it and the sea.
Hedges of butter fenced it round,
Under a crest of white-mantled lard
    Around the wall outside.

A row of fragrant apple-trees,
An orchard in its pink-tipped bloom,

Between it and the hill.
A forest tall of real leeks,
Of onions and of carrots, stood
Behind the house.

Within, a household generous,
A welcome of red, firm-fed men,
Around the fire:
Seven bead-strings and necklets seven
Of cheeses and of bits of tripe
Round each man's neck.

The Chief in cloak of beefy fat
Beside his noble wife and fair
I then beheld.
Below the lofty caldron's spit
Then the Dispenser I beheld,
His fleshfork on his back.

Wheatlet son of Milklet,
Son of juicy Bacon,
Is mine own name.
Honeyed Butter-roll
Is the man's name
That bears my bag.

Haunch of Mutton
Is my dog's name,
Of lovely leaps.
Lard, my wife,
Sweetly smiles
Across the brose.

Cheese-curds, my daughter,
Goes round the spit,
 Fair is her fame.
Corned Beef is my son,
Who beams over a cloak,
  Enormous, of fat.

Savour of Savours
Is the name of my wife's maid:
Morning-early
Across New-milk Lake she went.

Beef-lard, my steed,
An excellent stallion
  That increases studs;
A guard against toil
Is the saddle of cheese
  Upon his back.

A large necklace of delicious cheese-curds
  Around his back;
His halter and his traces all
  Of fresh butter.

KUNO MEYER

The Viking Terror

Translated from the Irish (8th–9th century)

Bitter is the wind tonight
It tosses the ocean's white hair:
Tonight I fear not the fierce warriors
    of Norway
Coursing on the Irish Sea.

ALICE MILLIGAN (1880–1953)

When I Was a Little Girl

When I was a little girl,
In a garden playing
A thing was often said
To chide us delaying:

When after sunny hours,
At twilight's falling,
Down through the garden walks
Came our old nurse calling.

"Come in! for it's growing late,
And the grass will wet ye!
Come in! or when it's dark
The Fenians will get ye."

Then, at this dreadful news,
All helter-skelter,
The panic-struck little flock
Ran home for shelter.

And round the nursery fire
Sat still to listen,
Fifty bare toes on the hearth,
Ten eyes a-glisten.

To hear of a night in March,
And loyal folk waiting,
To see a great army of men
Come devastating.

An Army of Papists grim,
With a green flag o'er them,

Red-coats and black police
Flying before them.

But God (Who our nurse declared
Guards British dominions)
Sent down a fall of snow
And scattered the Fenians.

"But somewhere they're lurking yet,
Maybe they're near us,"
Four little hearts pit-a-pat
Thought "Can they hear us?"

Then the wind-shaken pane
Sounded like drumming;
"Oh!" they cried, "tuck us in,
The Fenians are coming!"

Four little pairs of hands
In the cots where she led those,
Over their frightened heads
Pulled up the bedclothes.

But one little rebel there,
Watching all with laughter,
Thought, "When the Fenians come
I'll rise and go after."

Wished she had been a boy
And a good deal older —
Able to walk for miles
With a gun on her shoulder.

Able to lift aloft
The Green Flag o'er them

(Red-coats and black police
Flying before them).

And, as she dropped asleep,
Was wondering whether
God, if they prayed to Him,
Would give fine weather.

JOHN MONTAGUE (1929–   )

The Trout
For Barrie Cooke

Flat on the bank I parted
Rushes to ease my hands
In the water without a ripple
And tilt them slowly downstream
To where he lay, light as a leaf,
In his fluid sensual dream.

Bodiless lord of creation
I hung briefly above him
Savouring my own absence
Senses expanding in the slow
Motion, the photographic calm
That comes before action.

As the curve of my hands
Swung under his body
He surged, with visible pleasure.
I was so preternaturally close

I could count every stipple
But still cast no shadow, until

The two palms crossed in a cage
Under the lightly pulsing gills.
Then (entering my own enlarged
Shape, which rode on the water)
I gripped. To this day I can
Taste his terror on my hands.

Murphy in Manchester

He wakes to a confused dream of boats, gulls,
And all his new present floats
Suddenly up to him on rocking rails.
Through that long first day
He trudges streets, tracks friends,
Stares open-mouthed at monuments
To manufacturers, sabered generals.
Passing a vegetable stall
With exposed fruits, he halts
To contemplate a knobbly potato
With excitement akin to love.
At lunchtime, in a cafeteria,
He finds his feet and hands
Enlarge, become like foreign lands.
A great city is darkness, noise
Through which bright girls move
Like burnished other children's toys.
Soon the whistling factory
Will lock him in:
Half-stirred memories and regrets
Drowning in that iron din.

Time Out

The donkey sat down on the roadside
Suddenly, as though tired of carrying
His cross. There was a varnish
Of sweat on his coat, and a fly
On his left ear. The tinker

Beating him finally gave in,
Sat on the grass himself, prying
His coat for his pipe. The donkey
(not beautiful but more fragile
than any swan, with his small
front hooves folded under him)
Gathered enough courage to raise
That fearsome head, lipping a daisy,
As if to say — slowly, contentedly —
Yes, there is a virtue in movement,
But only going so far, so fast,
Sucking the sweet grass of stubbornness.

THOMAS MOORE (1779–1852)

I Saw from the Beach

I saw from the beach, when the morning was shining,
    A bark o'er the waters move gloriously on;
I came when the sun from that beach was declining,
    The bark was still there, but the waters were gone.

And such is the fate of our life's early promise,
    So passing the spring-tide of joy we have known;
Each wave, that we danc'd on at morning, ebbs from us,
    And leaves us, at eve, on the bleak shore alone.

Ne'er tell me of glories, serenely adorning
    The close of our day, the calm eve of our night; —
Give me back, give me back the wild freshness of Morning,
    Her clouds and her tears are worth Evening's best light.

The Time I've Lost in Wooing

The time I've lost in wooing
In watching and pursuing
  The light that lies
  In woman's eyes,
Has been my heart's undoing.
Though Wisdom oft has sought me,
I scorned the lore she brought me,
  My only books
  Were woman's looks,
And folly's all they've taught me.

Her smile when Beauty granted,
I hung with gaze enchanted,
  Like him the Sprite,
  Whom maids by night
Oft meet in glen that's haunted.
Like him, too, Beauty won me,
But while her eyes were on me,
  If once their ray
  Was turned away,
O, winds could not outrun me.

And are those follies going?
And is my proud heart growing
  Too cold or wise
  For brilliant eyes
Again to set it glowing?
No, vain, alas! th' endeavour
From bonds so sweet to sever; —
  Poor Wisdom's chance
  Against a glance
Is now as weak as ever.

Oft, in the Stilly Night

Oft, in the stilly night,
  Ere Slumber's chain has bound me,
Fond Memory brings the light
  Of other days around me;
    The smiles, the tears
    Of boyhood's years,
  The words of love then spoken;
    The eyes that shone,
    Now dimm'd and gone,
  The cheerful hearts now broken!
Thus, in the stilly night,
  Ere Slumber's chain has bound me,
Sad Memory brings the light
  Of other days around me.

When I remember all
  The friends, so link'd together,
I've seen around me fall
  Like leaves in wintry weather;
    I feel like one
    Who treads alone
  Some banquet-hall deserted,
    Whose lights are fled,
    Whose garlands dead,
  And all but he departed!
Thus, in the stilly night,
  Ere Slumber's chain has bound me,
Sad Memory brings the light
  Of other days around me.

Lying

I do confess, in many a sigh
My lips have breath'd you many a lie.
And who, with such delights in view,
Would lose them, for a lie or two?
Nay—look not thus, with brow reproving;
Lies are, my dear, the soul of loving!
If half we tell the girls were true,
If half we swear to think and do,
Were aught but lying's bright illusion,
The world would be in strange confusion!
If ladies' eyes were, every one,
As lover's swear, a radiant sun,
Astronomy should leave the skies,
To learn her lore in ladies' eyes!
Oh, no!—believe me, lovely girl,
When Nature turns your teeth to pearl,
Your neck to snow, your eyes to fire,
Your yellow locks to golden wire,
Then, only then, can Heaven decree,
That you should live for only me.

And now, my gentle hints to clear,
For once, I'll tell you truth, my dear!
Whenever you may chance to meet
A loving youth, whose love is sweet,
Long as you're false and he believes you,
Long as you trust and he deceives you,
So long the blissful bond endures;
And while he lies, his heart is yours:
But, oh! you've wholly lost the youth
The instant that he tells you truth!

RICHARD MURPHY (1927–   )

Droit de Seigneur
1820

In a grey rectory a clergyman was reading
Fortunate by firelight the *Connaught Journal.*
The shutters were closed, for famine was spreading
Among the people. The portrait of Cromwell,
One hand on the Bible, the other on a sword,
Had been stowed that evening under a haystack.
The air was crackling with the whips of rhetoric.

A groom was saddling his mare in the stable
While a redcoat stumbled down the loft ladder
Buttoning his tunic, followed by a girl
Who ran to the kitchen. The yard lantern
Yellowed the stirrups and the buckled leather
On the mare's girth as he combed her down.
The master was for hunting the Ribbonmen:

A secret band, swearing oaths by moonlight,
Refusing to pay tithes or rent to the landlord,
Who battered on lonely doors after midnight,
And wore round their sleeves a white riband.
He called it his duty to commit these rogues
To the jury of gentlemen at Galway Assizes.
Saving of property went with saving of souls.

So he galloped out with a few soldiers
On to the gravelled road under the lime-trees
With his father's pistol in a handsome holster.
They ambushed a wedding from the next parish.
All escaped except a young simpleton
In whose pocket they found a white bandage.
Twenty miles to Galway he was marched in chains.

In the pigeon park the heifers were grazing
Under the beech-trees. The soldiers had gone.
Behind the frown of the windows, browsing
On the price of cattle in the *Connaught Journal,*
The rector looked out on the frost and the sun.
The girl ran across the yard with a bucket.
"Tomorrow," he read, "the boy will be executed."

T. D. O'BOLGER

The Counsels of O'Riordan, the Rann Maker

The choirs of Heaven are tokened in a harp-string,
A pigeon's egg is as crafty as the stars.
My heart is shaken by the crying of the lap-wing,
And yet the world is full of foolish wars.

There's gold on the whin-bush every summer morning.
There's struggling discourse in the grunting of a pig:
Yet churls will be scheming, and churls will be scorning,
And half the dim world is ruled by thimble-rig.

The luck of God is in two strangers meeting,
But the gates of Hell are in the city street
For him whose soul is not in his own keeping
And love a silver string upon his feet.

My heart is the seed of time, my veins are star-dust,
My spirit is the axle of God's dream.
Why should my august soul be worn or care-tost? . . .
Lo, God is but a lamp, and I his gleam.

[*Rann:* a verse; a saying]

There's little to be known, and that not kindly,
But an ant will burrow through a two-foot wall;
There's nothing rises up or falls down blindly:
That's a poor share of wisdom, but it's all.

FRANK O'CONNOR (1903–1966)

Three Old Brothers

While some go dancing reels and some
   Go stuttering love in ditches
The three old brothers rise from bed,
   And moan, and pin their breeches;
And one says, "I can sleep no more,
   I'd liefer far go weeping,
For how should honest men lie still
   When brats can spoil their sleeping?"
And blind Tom says, that's eighty years,
   "If I was ten years younger
I'd take a stick and welt their rumps
   And gall their gamest runner!"
But James the youngest cries, "Praise God,
   We have outlived our passion!"
And by their fire of roots all three
   Praise God after a fashion.

Says James, "I loved when I was young
   A lass of one and twenty
That had the grace of all the queens
   And broke men's hearts in plenty,
But now the girl's a gammy crone

With no soft sides or boosom,
And all the lads she kist's abed
  Where the fat worm chews 'em;
And though she had no kiss for me,
  And though myself is older,
And though my thighs are cold tonight,
  Their thighs I think are colder!"

And Blind Tom says, "I knew a man
  A girl refused for lover
Worked in America forty years
  And heaped copper on copper,
And came back all across the foam,
  Dressed in his silks and satins,
And watched for her from dawn to dark
  And from Compline to Matins,
And when she passed him in her shawl
  He cracked his sides for laughing,
And went back happy to the west
  And heeded no man's scoffing,
And Christ!" moans Tom, "if I'd his luck
  I'd not mind cold nor coughing!"

Says Patcheen then, "My lot's a lot
  All men on earth might envy,
That saw the girl I could not get
  Nurse an untimely baby!"
And all three say, "Dear heart! Dear heart!"
  And James the youngest mutters,
"Praise God we have outlived our griefs
  And not fell foul like others,
Like Paris and the Grecian chiefs
  And the three Ulster brothers!"

The Harper
Translated from the Irish (17th century)

Master of discords John
  Makes harmony seem wrong,
His treble sings to his bass
  Like a sow consoling her young.

If he played with his shoulder-blades
  'Twould yield a pleasanter tone,
He reaches out for a chord
  As a dog snaps at a bone.

Playing away to himself
  God only knows what tune,
Even the man who made it
  Cannot recall his own.

A wonder the way he works
  He never keeps tune or time,
With skill and care he goes wrong,
  Mountains of error climb.

Give him the simplest catch
  And at once you're in at the kill,
He mangles it patiently
  Like an old loud derelict mill.

Copper scratched with a knife,
  Brass cut with a rasp,
His nails scrape at the strings
  Till all shudder and gasp.

God help you gentle harp
  Pounded and plagued by his fist,
There isn't a chord in your breast
  Without a sprain or twist.

A Man of Experience
  Translated from the Irish of Laoiseach Mac an Bhaird

  Really, what a shocking scene!
    A decent girl, a public place!
  What the devil do you mean,
    Mooching round with such a face?

Things can't really be so bad,
   Surely someone would have said
If — of course the thing is mad,
   No, your mother isn't dead.

Sighing, sniffling, looking tense,
   Sitting mum the whole day through;
Speaking from experience
   I can guess what's wrong with you.

Roses withering in the cheek,
   Sunlight clouding in the hair,
Heaving breasts and looks so meek —
   You're in love, my girl, I swear.

If love really caused all this
   So that looks and grace are gone
Shouldn't you tell me who it is? —
   Even if I should be the man.

If I really were the man
   You woldn't find me too severe,
Don't think I'm a Puritan,
   I've been through it too my dear.

And if you'd whispered in my ear:
   "Darling, I'm in love with you"
I wouldn't have scolded, never fear;
   I know just what girls go through.

How does it take you, could you say?
   Are you faint when I pass by?
Don't just blush and look away —
   Who should know love if not I?

You'll be twice the girl tonight
　　Once you get it off your chest;
Why—who knows?—you even might
　　Win me to your snowy breast.

Make love just the way that seems
　　Fittest to you, 'twill be right.
Think of it! Your wildest dreams
　　Might come true this very night.

That's enough for once, my dear
　　Stop that snivelling and begin;
Come now, not another tear—
　　Lord, look at the state you're in!

Kilcash

Translated from the Irish (17th century)

What shall we do for timber?
　　The last of the woods is down.
Kilcash and the house of its glory
　　And the bell of the house are gone,
The spot where that lady waited
　　Who shamed all women for grace
When earls came sailing to greet her
　　And Mass was said in the place.

My grief and my affliction
　　Your gates are taken away,
Your avenue needs attention,
　　Goats in the garden stray.
The courtyard's filled with water
　　And the great earls where are they?

The earls, the lady, the people
   Beaten into the clay.

No sound of duck or geese there,
   Hawk's cry or eagle's call,
No humming of the bees there
   That brought honey and wax for all,
Nor even the song of the birds there
   When the sun goes down in the west,
No cuckoo on top of the boughs there,
   Singing the world to rest.

There's mist there tumbling from branches,
   Unstirred by night and by day,
And darkness falling from heaven,
   For our fortune has ebbed away,
There's no holly nor hazel nor ash there,
   The pasture's rock and stone,
The crown of the forest has withered,
   And the last of its game is gone.

I beseech of Mary and Jesus
   That the great come home again
With long dances danced in the garden,
   Fiddle music and mirth among men,
That Kilcash the home of our fathers
   Be lifted on high again,
And from that to the deluge of waters
   In bounty and peace remain.

[NOTE: In 1691 the English destroyed all woodlands because they hid the rebellious army of Patrick Sarsfield.]

SEÁN O'CRÍADÁIN (1930–   )

Great-Aunts

Living in an old house
With old furniture and books
And even older, ancient women
Held youth intact,
Softened the impact
Of being seventeen
And very, very wise.

EUGENE O'CURRY (1796–1862)

Do You Remember That Night?
Translated from the Irish (17th century)

Do you remember that night
When you were at the window,
With neither hat nor gloves
Nor coat to shelter you?
I reached out my hand to you,
And you ardently grasped it;
I remained to converse with you
Until the lark began to sing.

Do you remember that night
That you and I were
At the foot of the rowan tree,
And the night drifting snow?
Your head on my breast,
And your pipe sweetly playing?
Little thought I that night
That our love ties would loosen!

Beloved of my inmost heart,
Come some night and soon,
When my people are at rest,
That we may talk together.
My arms shall encircle you
While I relate my sad tale,
That your soft, pleasant converse
Hath deprived me of heaven.

The fire is unraked,
The light unextinguished,
The key under the door,
Do you softly draw it.
My mother is asleep,
But I am wide awake;
My fortune in my hand,
I am ready to go with you.

SEAN O'FAOLAIN (1900–   )

Summer is Gone
Translated from the Irish (9th century)

I have but one story—
The stags are moaning,
The sky is snowing,
Summer is gone.

Quickly the low sun
Goes drifting down
Behind the rollers,
Lifting and long.

The wild geese cry
Down the storm;
The ferns have fallen,
Russet and torn.

The wings of the birds
Are clotted with ice.
I have but one story —
Summer is gone.

DESMOND O'GRADY (1935–   )

Afternoon

Afternoon, and the houses are quiet as dust at the foot
   of a wall.
The tea and the coffee things cleared away from the talk
   and the thinking,
The magazines flicked through, the telephone tempting,
   the sand in the hourglass sinking.
The waiting – knowing nothing will happen at all.

Afternoon, and just for the want of something more dar-
   ing to do
Lunch is being digested in the serious bowels of the town.
The buses are empty, the taxis unwanted and lorries are
   caught in a brown
Study of idleness. Business is slow.

In the parks and the playgrounds, shifty-eyed watchers
   in colourless clothes
Are hanging around like agents of death, while profes-
   sional loungers,
In soft hats and silence, disinterestedly wait for the next
   observation; and scroungers
And tricksters are nervously watching what goes.

Down by the shipless, motionless docks; abandoned by all
Except for a stray indefinable blur of what must be a man
And the inevitable rake of a pigeon scratching for corn;
   the cranes
Are struck dead – unable even to fall.

The voice on the radio — remote, unmelodic — gives news
    of events
And things that are happening — urban expansion, rural
    improvements,
Revolutions and riots, social reforms and new intellectual
    movements —
In lands with more futures than this one presents.

In the lanes and the archways the children are few — the
    lovers fewer still;
And those who are left have plans and intentions of join-
    ing the rest
On emigrant tickets. In the streets there is no one but old
    men and widows, cursed
With sorry separation and a broken will.

Crack, and the shouts of men go up as a rat breaks cover
To die by the stones and the longhandled sticks of exas-
    peration,
Back of the wagons in the stopped yards of the black,
    uneventful station —
And just for a moment the waiting is over.

MOIRA O'NEILL (1863–1955)

The Rachray Man

Och, what was it got me at all that time
To promise I'd marry a Rachray man?
An' now he'll not listen to rason or rhyme,
He's strivin' to hurry me all that he can.
   "Come on, an' ye *be* to come on!" says he,
   "Ye're bound for the Island, to live wi' me."

See Rachray Island beyont in the bay,
An' the dear knows what they be doin' out there
But fishin' an' fightin' an' tearin' away,
An' who's to hindher, an' what do they care?
   The goodness can tell what 'ud happen to me
   When Rachray 'ud have me, *anee, anee!*

I might have took Pether from over the hill,
A dacent poacher, the kind poor boy:
Could I keep the ould places about me still
I'd never set foot out o' sweet Ballyvoy.
   My sorra on Rachray, the could sea-caves,
   An' blackneck divers, an' weary ould waves!

I'll never win back now, whatever may fall,
So give me good luck, for ye'll see me no more;
Sure an Island man is the mischief an' all —
An' me that never was married before!
   Oh think o' my fate when ye dance at a fair,
   In Rachray there' no Christianity there.

ARTHUR O'SHAUGHNESSY (1844–1881)

Ode

We are the music-makers,
　And we are the dreamers of dreams,
Wandering by lone sea-breakers,
　And sitting by desolate streams; —

World-losers and world-forsakers,
　On whom the pale moon gleams:
Yet we are the movers and shakers
　Of the world for ever, it seems.

With wonderful deathless ditties
We build up the world's great cities,
　And out of a fabulous story
　We fashion an empire's glory:

One man with a dream, at pleasure,
　Shall go forth and conquer a crown;
And three with a new song's measure
　Can trample an empire down.

We, in the ages lying
　In the buried past of the earth,
Built Nineveh with our sighing,
　And Babel itself with our mirth;
And o'erthrew them with prophesying
　To the old of the new world's worth;
For each age is a dream that is dying,
　Or one that is coming to birth.

D. J. O'SULLIVAN (1906–   )

Drinking Time

Two black heifers and a red
Standing on the river-bed,
Filling up their belly-tanks,
Water swirling 'round their flanks.

In the stirred-up river mud
Elvers wriggle, flat-fish scud;
Where the torrent's slow and deep
Sea-bound smolt lie half-asleep.

Buzzing flies bite bovine flesh,
Twitching tails make rainbow-splash,
One black sucks a tadpole in,
Sniffs and snorts create a din.

Now the farmer's voice is heard
Above the cymbal-tinkling ford,
"Bramble, Bluebell, Buttercup;
Hi, come out, come cow — up!"

In answer to the urging call
They leave for shelter'd byre stall,
Oaten mash and hay-strewn bed,
Two black heifers and a red.

SEUMAS O'SULLIVAN (1879–1958)

Cottage

As the candle light and fire light
Weave patterns on the rafters overhead,
And on the couples advancing,
In light and shadow, all in shadow some,
The little crooked fiddler, apple-red,
Smiles at the prospect of long drinks to come.

Rain
(*Donegal*)

All day long
The grey rain beating,
On the bare hills
Where the scant grass cannot cover,
The grey rocks peeping
Through the salt herbage.
All day long
The young lambs bleating
Stand for covering
Where the scant grass is
Under the grey wall,
Or seeking softer shelter
Under tattered fleeces
Nuzzle the warm udders.
All day long
The little waves leaping
Round the grey rocks
By the brown tide borders,
Round the black headlands
Streaming with rain.

A Blessing on the Cows

My blessing on the patient cows,
Long life, and gentle death—and then
May they on heavenly meadows browse,
Breathing sweet breath into sweet grass,
Fragrance to fragrance, even as when
I see them daily where I pass
On the sweet upland pasture browse;
My blessing on the patient cows.

The Convent

The rooks above the convent walls
Are mating in the trees.
The nuns, within the convent gloom
Are praying on their knees.
O nuns upon your bended knees,
How can you really hope to please
The god of sky and sun and breeze,
Of mating birds, and burgeoning trees
By praying on your bended knees
Within a darkened room?

A Piper

A piper in the street today,
Set up, and tuned, and started to play,
And away, away, away on the tide
Of his music we started; on every side
Doors and windows were opened wide,

And men left down their work and came,
And women with petticoats coloured like flame,
And little bare feet that were blue with cold,
Went dancing back to the age of gold,
And all the world went gay, went gay,
For half an hour in the street today.

BASIL PAYNE (1928–   )

Angry Old Men

Those days, the angry persons were the old:
Killarney, for instance (so we christened him),
An old man with a long and yellow beard,
Who, at exactly two o'clock each Tuesday,
Sang "By Killarney's Lakes" outside our house
— My father often set his watch by him.
He never knocked for alms; but roared abuse
And shook his walking stick at us, when we
Mocked him with our soprano schoolboy chorus:
Until, one Tuesday, he did not turn up:
— None of us ever heard what happened to him.

Next, there was Damn the Weather; less predictable
Than old Killarney, and more violent;
He would come stamping down the street in boots
A size too big for him, and leather leggings
— A swearing, one-man army on the march.
Winter or summer, purple-faced, he'd shout
"Damn the weather; damn the bloody weather!"
— "Shell-shock," my mother patiently explained.

The Blind Man came on Sundays: him alone
The rules secured from children's mockery.
I did not like him; pounding on each door
Aggressively, he'd order "Help the Blind!",
Adding "God Bless You," when he got his coin.
(None of our parents ever dared refuse.)

PADRAIC PEARSE (1879-1916)

Last Lines — 1916
(*Written the night before his execution*)

The beauty of the world hath made me sad,
This beauty that will pass;
Sometimes my heart hath shaken with great joy
To see a leaping squirrel in a tree,
Or a red lady-bird upon a stalk,
Or little rabbits in a field at evening,
Lit by a slanting sun,
Or some green hill where shadows drifted by,
Some quiet hill where mountainy man hath sown
And soon would reap; near to the gate of Heaven;
Or children with bare feet upon the sands
Of some ebbed sea, or playing on the streets
Of little towns in Connacht,
Things young and happy.
And then my heart hath told me:
These will pass,
Will pass and change, will die and be no more,
Things bright and green, things young and happy;
And I have gone upon my way
Sorrowful.

JOSEPH MARY PLUNKETT (1887–1916)

1867

All our best ye have branded
When the people were choosing them,
When 'twas Death they demanded
Ye laughed! Ye were losing them.
But the blood that ye spilt in the night
Crieth loudly to God,
And their name hath the strength and the might
Of a sword for the sod.

In the days of our doom and our dread
Ye were cruel and callous,
Grim Death with our fighters ye fed
Through the jaws of the gallows;
But a blasting and blight was the fee
For which ye had bartered them,
And we smite with the sword that from ye
We had gained when ye martyred them!

W. R. RODGERS (1909–1969)

White Christmas

Punctually at Christmas the soft plush
Of sentiment snows down, embosoms all
The sharp and pointed shapes of venom, shawls
The hills and hides the shocking holes of this
Uneven world of want and wealth, cushions

With cosy wish like cotton-wool the cool
Arm's-length interstices of caste and class,
And into obese folds subtracts from sight
All truculent acts, bleeding the world white.

Punctually that glib pair, Peace and Goodwill,
Emerges royally to take the air,
Collect the bows, assimilate the smiles,
Of waiting men. It is a genial time;
Angels, like stalactites, descend from heaven;
Bishops distribute their own weight in words,
Congratulate the poor on Christlike lack;
And the member for the constituency
Feeds the five thousand, and has plenty back.

Punctually, tonight, in old stone circles
Of set reunion, families stiffly sit
And listen: this is the night and this the happy time
When the tinned milk of human kindness is
Upheld and holed by radio-appeal:
Hushed are hurrying heels on hard roads,
And every parlour's a pink pond of light
To the cold and travelling man going by
In the dark, without a bark or a bite.

But punctually tomorrow you will see
All this silent and dissembling world
Of stilted sentiment suddenly melt
Into mush and watery welter of words
Beneath the warm and moving traffic of
Feet and actual fact. Over the stark plain
The silted mill-chimneys once again spread
Their sackcloth and ashes, a flowing mane
Of repentance for the false day that's fled.

The Fountains

Suddenly all the fountains in the park
Opened smoothly their umbrellas of water,
Yet there was none but me to miss or mark
Their peacock show, and so I moved away
Uneasily, like one who at a play
Finds himself all alone, and will not stay.

Armagh

There is a through-otherness about Armagh
Of tower and steeple,
Up on the hill are the arguing graves of the kings,
And below are the people.

Through-other as the rooks that swoop and swop
Over the sober hill
Go the people gallivanting from shop to shop
Guffawing their fill.

And the little houses run through the market town
Slap up against the great,
Like the farmers all clabber and muck walking arm by
    arm
With the men of estate.

Raised at a time when Reason was all the rage,
Of grey and equal stone,
This bland face of Armagh covers an age
Of clay and feather and bone.

Through-other is its history, of Celt and Dane,
Norman and Saxon,

Who ruled the place and sounded the gamut of fame
From cow-horn to klaxon.

There is a through-otherness about Armagh
Delightful to me,
Up on the hill are the graves of the garrulous kings
Who at last can agree.

THOMAS WILLIAM ROLLESTON (1857–1920)

The Dead at Clonmacnoise
Translated from the Irish

In a quiet water'd land, a land of roses,
    Stands Saint Kieran's city fair;
And the warriors of Erin in their famous generations
    Slumber there.

There beneath the dewy hillside sleep the noblest
    Of the clan of Conn,
Each below his stone with name in branching Ogham
    And the sacred knot thereon.

There they laid to rest the seven Kings of Tara,
    There the sons of Cairbré sleep —
Battle-banners of the Gael, that in Kieran's plain of
    crosses
    Now their final hosting keep.

And in Clonmacnoise they laid the men of Teffia,
    And right many a lord of Breagh;
Deep the sod above Clan Creidé and Clan Conaill,
    Kind in hall and fierce in fray.

Many and many a son of Conn, the Hundred-Fighter,
  In the red earth lies at rest;
Many a blue eye of Clan Colman the turf covers,
  Many a swan-white breast.

GEORGE WILLIAM RUSSELL (AE) (1867–1935)

The Vesture of the Soul

I pitied one whose tattered dress
Was patched, and stained with dust and rain;
He smiled on me; I could not guess
The viewless spirit's wide domain.

He said, "The royal robe I wear
Trails all along the fields of light:
Its silent blue and silver bear
For gems the starry dust of night.

"The breath of Joy unceasingly
Waves to and fro its folds starlit,
And far beyond earth's misery
I live and breathe the joy of it."

RICHARD RYAN (1946–   )

The Thrush's Nest
For Michael Kinsella

Bramble, like barbed wire,
Stitches the thicket tight, laces
A net of leaves against the
Light: only the birds can pass.

Pinned high where the twigs
Cross, it shapes from a blur;
Still heart of the bush, darkness
Parts slowly to let it through.

Her black pebble-eyes dazed
With waiting, the mother snaps
Alive at my presence, grabs
Air, screaming — reveals her shining

Hoard: luminous with heat,
Four freckled ovals of perfect
Sky, the skin of one threaded
With cracks — pulsing with life.

JAMES STEPHENS (1881–1950)

The Centaurs

Playing upon the hill three centaurs were!
They lifted each a hoof! They stared at me!
And stamped the dust!

They stamped the dust! They snuffed upon the air!
And all their movements had the fierce glee
Of power, and pride, and lust!

Of power and pride and lust! Then, with a shout,
They tossed their heads, and wheeled, and galloped
    round,
In furious brotherhood!

In furious brotherhood! Around, about,
They charged, they swerved, they leaped! Then, bound
    on bound,
They raced into the wood!

Nora Criona

I have looked him round and looked him through,
Know everything that he will do

In such a case, and such a case;
And when a frown comes on his face

I dream of it, and when a smile
I trace its sources in a while.

He cannot do a thing but I
Peep to find the reason why;

For I love him, and I seek,
Every evening in the week,

To peep behind his frowning eye
With little query, little pry,

And make him, if a woman can,
Happier than any man.

— Yesterday he gripped her tight
And cut her throat. And serve her right!

The Wind

The wind stood up, and gave a shout;
He whistled on his fingers, and

Kicked the withered leaves about,
And thumped the branches with his hand,

And said he'd kill, and kill, and kill;
And so he will! And so he will!

Bessie Bobtail

As down the road she wambled slow,
She had not got a place to go:
She had not got a place to fall
And rest herself—no place at all:
She stumped along, and wagged her pate;
And said a thing was desperate.

Her face was screwed and wrinkled tight
Just like a nut—and, left and right,
On either side, she wagged her head
And said a thing; and what she said
Was desperate as any word
That ever yet a person heard.

I walked behind her for a while,
And watched the people nudge and smile:
But ever, as she went, she said,
As left and right she swung her head,
—*Oh, God He knows! And, God He knows!*
And, surely God Almighty knows!

The Devil's Bag

I saw the Devil walking down the lane
Behind our house. — A heavy bag
Was strapped upon his shoulders and the rain
Sizzled when it hit him.
He picked a rag
Up from the ground and put it in his sack,
And grinned, and rubbed his hands.
There was a thing
Alive inside the bag upon his back
— It must have been a soul! I saw it fling
And twist about inside, and not a hole
Or cranny for escape! Oh, it was sad!
I cried, and shouted out, — *Let out that soul!* —
But he turned round, and, sure, his face went mad,
And twisted up and down, and he said *"Hell!"*
And ran away . . . Oh, mammy! I'm not well.

To the Four Courts, Please

The driver rubbed at his nettly chin
With a huge loose forefinger, crooked and black;
And his wobbly violet lips sucked in,
And puffed out again and hung down slack:
A black fang shone through his lop-sided smile,
In his little pouched eye flickered years of guile.

And the horse, poor beast! It was ribbed and forked;
And its ears hung down, and its eyes were old;
And its knees were knuckly; and, as we talked,
It swung the stiff neck that could scarcely hold
Its big skinny head up — then I stepped in,
And the driver climbed to his seat with a grin.

God help the horse, and the driver too!
And the people and beasts who have never a friend!
For the driver easily might have been you,
And the horse be me by a different end!
And nobody knows how their days will cease!
And the poor, when they're old, have little of peace!

The County Mayo
Translated from the Irish of Anthony Raftery
(c. 1784–1835)

Now with the coming in of the spring the days will stretch
a bit,
And after the Feast of Brigid I shall hoist my flag and go,
For since the thought got into my head I can neither
stand nor sit
Until I find myself in the middle of the County of Mayo.

In Claremorris I would stop a night and sleep with decent
men,
And then go on to Balla just beyond and drink galore,
And next to Kiltimagh for a visit of about a month, and
then
I would only be a couple of miles away from Ballymore.

I say and swear my heart lifts up like the lifting of a tide,
Rising up like the rising wind till fog or mist must go,
When I remember Carra and Gallen close beside,
And the Gap of the Two Bushes, and the wide plains of
Mayo.

To Killaden then, to the place where everything grows
that is best,

There are raspberries there and strawberries there and
all that is good for men;
And if I were only there in the middle of my folk my heart
could rest,
For age itself would leave me there and I'd be young
again.

I Am Raftery
Translated from the Irish of Anthony Raftery

I am Raftery the poet,
Full of hope and love,
My eyes without sight,
My mind without torment,

Going west on my journey
By the light of my heart,
Tired and weary
To the end of the road.

Behold me now
With my back to a wall,
Playing music
To empty pockets.

L. A. G. STRONG (1896–1958)

A Memory

When I was as high as that
I saw a poet in his hat.
I think the poet must have smiled
At such a solemn gazing child.

Now wasn't it a funny thing
To get a sight of J. M. Synge,
And notice nothing but his hat?
Yet life is often queer like that.

L. A. G. STRONG

The Mad-Woman

Aswell within her billowed skirts
   Like a great ship with sails unfurled,
The mad-woman goes gallantly
   Upon the ridges of her world.

With eagle nose and wisps of grey
   She strides upon the westward hills,
Swings her umbrella joyously
   And waves it to the waving mills,

Talking and chuckling as she goes
   Indifferent both to sun and rain,
With all that merry company
   The singing children of her brain.

The Knowledgeable Child

I always see, — I don't know why, —
If any person's going to die.

That's why nobody talks to me.
There was a man who came to tea,

And when I saw that he would die
I went to him and said "Good-bye,

"I shall not see you any more."
He died that evening. Then, next door,

They had a little girl: she died
Nearly as quick, and Mummy cried

And cried, and ever since that day
She's made me promise not to say.

But folks are still afraid of me,
And, where they've children, nobody

Will let me next or nigh to them
For fear I'll say good-bye to them.

JONATHAN SWIFT (1667–1745)

On Himself

On rainy days alone I dine
Upon a chick and pint of wine.
On rainy days I dine alone
And pick my chicken to the bone;
But this my servants much enrages,
No scraps remain to save board-wages.
In weather fine I nothing spend,
But often spunge upon a friend;
Yet, where he's not so rich as I,
I pay my club, and so good-bye.

Market Women's Cries

APPLES

Come buy my fine wares,
Plums, apples and pears.
A hundred a penny,
In conscience too many:
Come, will you have any?
My children are seven,
I wish them in Heaven;
My husband 's a sot,
With his pipe and his pot,
Not a farthen will gain them,
And I must maintain them.

HERRINGS

Be not sparing,
Leave off swearing.
Buy my herring
Fresh from Malahide,
Better never was tried.
Come, eat them with pure fresh butter and mustard,
Their bellies are soft, and as white as a custard.
Come, sixpence a dozen, to get me some bread,
Or, like my own herrings, I soon shall be dead.

ONIONS

Come, follow me by the smell,
Here are delicate onions to sell;
I promise to use you well.
They make the blood warmer,
You'll feed like a farmer;
For this is every cook's opinion,
No savoury dish without an onion;
But, lest your kissing should be spoiled,
Your onions must be thoroughly boiled:
Or else you may spare
Your mistress a share,
The secret will never be known:
She cannot discover
The breath of her lover,
But think it as sweet as her own.

JOHN MILLINGTON SYNGE (1871–1909)

In Glencullen

Thrush, linnet, stare, and wren,
Brown lark beside the sun,
Take thought of kestrel, sparrow-hawk,
Birdlime and roving gun.

You great-great-grandchildren
Of birds I've listened to,
I think I robbed your ancestors
When I was young as you.

A Question

I asked if I got sick and died, would you
With my black funeral go walking too,
If you'd stand close to hear them talk or pray
While I'm let down in that steep bank of clay.

And, No, you said, for if you saw a crew
Of living idiots pressing round that new
Oak coffin—they alive, I dead beneath
That board—you'd rave and rend them with your teeth.

Is It a Month

Is it a month since I and you
In the starlight of Glen Dubh
Stretched beneath a hazel bough
Kissed from ear and throat to brow,
Since your fingers, neck, and chin
Made the bars that fenced me in,
Till Paradise seemed but a wreck
Near your bosom, brow, and neck,
And stars grew wilder, growing wise,
In the splendour of your eyes!
Since the weasel wandered near
Whilst we kissed from ear to ear
And the wet and withered leaves
Blew about your cap and sleeves,
Till the moon sank tired through the ledge
Of the wet and windy hedge?
And we took the starry lane
Back to Dublin town again.

Patch-Shaneen

Shaneen and Maurya Prendergast
Lived west in Carnareagh,
And they'd a cur-dog, cabbage plot,
A goat, and cock of hay.

He was five foot one or two,
Herself was four foot ten,
And he went travelling asking meal
Above through Caragh Glen.

She'd pick her bag of carrageen
Or perries through the surf,
Or loan an ass of Foxy Jim
To fetch her creel of turf.

Till on one windy Samhain night,
When there's stir among the dead,
He found her perished, stiff and stark,
Beside him in the bed.

And now when Shaneen travels far
From Droum to Ballyhyre
The women lay him sacks or straw,
Beside the seed of fire.

And when the grey cocks crow and flap,
And winds are in the sky,
"Oh, Maurya, Maurya, are you dead?"
You'll hear Patch-Shaneen cry.

JOHN TODHUNTER (1839–1916)

Aghadoe

There's a glen in Aghadoe, Aghadoe, Aghadoe,
There's a green and silent glade in Aghadoe,
   Where we met, my Love and I, Love's fair planet in
    the sky,
O'er that sweet and silent glen in Aghadoe.

There's a glen in Aghadoe, Aghadoe, Aghadoe,
There's a deep and secret glen in Aghadoe,
   Where I hid him from the eyes of the redcoats and
    their spies
That year the trouble came to Aghadoe!

Oh! my curse on one black heart in Aghadoe, Aghadoe,
On Shaun Dhuv, my mother's son in Aghadoe,
    When your throat fries in hell's drouth salt the flame
      be in your mouth,
For the treachery you did in Aghadoe!

For they tracked me to that glen in Aghadoe, Aghadoe,
When the price was on his head in Aghadoe;
    O'er the mountain through the wood, as I stole to him
      with food,
When in hiding low he lay in Aghadoe.

But they never took him living in Aghadoe, Aghadoe;
With the bullets in his heart in Aghadoe,
    There he lay, the head — my breast keeps the warmth
      where once 'twould rest —
Gone, to win the traitor's gold from Aghadoe!

I walked to Mallow Town from Aghadoe, Aghadoe,
Brought his head from the jail's gate to Aghadoe,
    Then I covered him with fern, and I piled on him the
      cairn,
Like an Irish king he sleeps in Aghadoe.

[*Shaun Dhuv:* Black-haired John]

HERBERT TRENCH (1865–1923)

Jean Richepin's Song

A poor lad once and a lad so trim,
  (*Fol de rol de raly O!*
    Fol de rol!)
A poor lad once and a lad so trim
Gave his love to her that loved not him.

And, says she, "Fetch me tonight, you rogue,"
  (*Fol de rol de raly O!*
    Fol de rol!)
And, says she, "Fetch me tonight, you rogue,
Your mother's heart to feed my dog!"

To his mother's house went that young man,
  (*Fol de rol de raly O!*
    Fol de rol!)
To his mother's house went that young man,
Killed her, and took the heart, and ran.

And as he was running, look you, he fell,
  (*Fol de rol de raly O!*
    Fol de rol!)
And as he was running, look you, he fell,
And the heart rolled on the ground as well.

And the lad, as the heart was a-rolling, heard
  (*Fol de rol de raly, O!*
    Fol de rol!)
And the lad, as the heart was a-rolling, heard
That the heart was speaking, and this was the word —

The heart was a-weeping, and crying so small
  (*Fol de rol de raly O!*
    Fol de rol!)
The heart was a-weeping and crying so small,
"Are you hurt, my child, are you hurt at all?"

JOHN FRANCIS WALLER (1810–1894)

The Spinning Wheel

Mellow the moonlight to shine is beginning,
Close by the window young Eileen is spinning;
Bent over the fire her blind grandmother, sitting,
Is crooning, and moaning, and drowsily knitting:—
"Eileen, achora, I hear someone tapping."
"'Tis the ivy, dear mother, against the glass flapping."
"Eily, I surely hear somebody sighing."
"'Tis the sound, mother dear, of the summer wind dy-
    ing."
Merrily, cheerily, noiselessly whirring,
Swings the wheel, spins the wheel, while the foot's stir-
    ring;
Sprightly, and brightly, and airily ringing
Thrills the sweet voice of the young maiden singing.

"What's that noise that I hear at the window, I wonder?"
"'Tis the little birds chirping the holly-bush under."
"What makes you be shoving and moving your stool on,
And singing, all wrong, that old song of "The Coolun'?"
There's a form at the casement—the form of her true
    love—
And he whispers, with face bent, "I'm waiting for you,
    love;
Get up on the stool, through the lattice step lightly,

We'll rove in the grove, while the moon's shining
    brightly."
Merrily, cheerily, noiselessly whirring,
Swings the wheel, spins the wheel, while the foot's stir-
    ring;
Sprightly, and brightly, and airily ringing
Thrills the sweet voice of the young maiden singing.

The maid shakes her head, on her lips lays her fingers,
Steals up from her seat—longs to go, and yet lingers;
A frightened glance turns to her drowsy grandmother,
Puts one foot on the stool, spins the wheel with the other,
Lazily, easily, swings now the wheel round,
Slowly and lowly is heard now the reel's sound;
Noiseless and light to the lattice above her
The maid steps—then leaps to the arms of her lover.
Slower—and slower—and slower the wheel swings;
Lower—and lower—and lower the reel rings;
Ere the reel and the wheel stopped their ringing and
    moving,
Through the grove the young lovers by moonlight are
    roving.

JOAN WATTON (1942–   )

Requiem of a War-Baby

I was born in August, 1942—conceived on a Christmas
    leave.
I know little of my father, having seen him just once,
    when I was three.
The room was dark and a turf fire burned.
I stood on one of the little boxes that clipped to each side
    of the fender.

And there were fruit gums and Mummy was happy and
   it was very quiet.
I didn't pay much attention to the tall man.
I think I preferred the sweets he had brought.

In the grim school years when it is so crucial to be the
   same as everyone else,
There were many flushed moments.
They knew so much more about him than I did.

I remember my last Christmas at the Primary.
It was snowing.
I hit one of the "enemies" with a hard snowball, as she
   was running to hide in the toilets.

Someone shouted to her, "Go home and tell your daddy,
   cry-baby."
"It's more than Joan Watton can do anyway," was the
   swift reply.
The snowball I was holding dropped from my hands.
I remember the hush, and the eyes.
I remember the whiteness, and the blood rising in my
   face.

The Head called us from the yard.
He slapped with a whippy cane on each outstretched
   frozen right hand.
My turn — "Betty Pedlow insulted me, sir."
I felt not so much the physical pain, but the injustice,
As the cane came down, first on one hand and then the
   other.

All through school I told the little fibs —
"Working in England, killed in the war. . . ."
Anything that sounded legitimate.

There was a browned photograph that was kept in a
    handbag on top of the wardrobe.
I would stand on a chair, and gape at the big, crew-cutted
    soldier —
Making myself hate him, because I felt I ought.

It wasn't until I was fifteen that they decided I was old
    enough to know.
"You see, Joan, he sent no money — he asked for a di-
    vorce, and then he wrote and said he had had a child
    to another woman —
And your Mammy had to go out to work and. . . ."
It was stark reality to have to swallow at that dreamy age.

But despite it all I wanted to meet him.
Then I found his letters — weak, weak . . .
With a tired disgust, my last curiosity thwarted.

It's easy to dramatize.
The absolute truth is, I am not all that much different
    from a daughter with a father.

RICHARD WEBER (1932–   )

Stephen's Green Revisited

The spring sun bends down between the branches.
The ducks continue with their cry of *aqua, aqua.*
Last autumn we came here for a little silence,
Our toes tempting the water, a breath of breeze
Hardly disturbing us; talked and were silent.
As in a picture, with everyone stopped in the act
Of moving or looking, a minute became an instant,

The world suddenly stilled in a midday haze of sun.
Even the ducks were silent, their bodies unmoving
Over unmoving reflections. Then slowly the world
Began to go again, and time helped us to our feet.
The ducks quickly recalled their little Latin
And their work of furrowing waves in the water.
Later your brown eyes watched me leave you sadly
But hopefully. Six months have passed since then
And we have said goodbye again in another city.
We have everything to hope for, yet I write sadly.
Memory is the mother of the muses, someone said.
But sadness is surely the secret mother of memory.

For the Moment

The wretched lost rejected lover
Who cries tears — and at his age;

The writer who stares all night,
White-faced, at the white page;

The paradoxical philosopher who discovers
That his reasons are not reasonable;

The hurt wife who picks at her hurt
Until it becomes a kind of heart-trouble:

All know that life cannot be good
Unless they should imagine death
Arriving for them at that moment.

Love, hate, life, reason, the instant
Of intake of another new breath,
Can then, in that moment, be understood.

LADY WILDE (1826–1896)

The Famine Year

Weary men, what reap ye? — "Golden corn for the
    stranger."
What sow ye? — "Human corses that wait for the avenger."
Fainting forms, hunger-stricken, what see ye in the offing?
"Stately ships to bear our food away amid the stranger's
    scoffing."
There's a proud array of soldiers — what do they round
    your door?
"They guard our master's granaries from the thin hands
    of the poor."
Pale mothers, wherefore weeping? "Would to God that
    we were dead —
Our children swoon before us, and we cannot give them
    bread!"

Little children, tears are strange upon your infant faces,
God meant you but to smile within your mother's soft
    embraces.
"Oh! we know not what is smiling, and we know not what
    is dying;
But we're hungry, very hungry, and we cannot stop our
    crying.
And some of us grow cold and white — we know not what
    it means;
But as they lie beside us we tremble in our dreams."
There's a gaunt crowd on the highway — are you come to
    pray to man,
With hollow eyes that cannot weep, and for words your
    faces wan?

"No; the blood is dead within our veins — we care not
    now for life;

Let us die hid in the ditches, far from children and from
wife!
We cannot stay to listen to their raving famished cries —
Bread! Bread! Bread! and none to still their agonies.
We left an infant playing with her dead mother's hand:
We left a maiden maddened by the fever's scorching
brand:"
Better, maiden, thou wert strangled in thy own dark-
twisted tresses!
Better, infant, thou wert smothered in thy mother's first
caresses.

"We are fainting in our misery, but God will hear our
groan;
Yet, if fellow-men desert us, will He hearken from His
throne?
Accursed are we in our own land, yet toil we still and
toil;
But the stranger reaps our harvest — the alien owns our
soil.
O Christ! how have we sinned, that on our native plains
We perish homeless, naked, starved, with branded brow
like Cain's?
Dying, dying wearily, with a torture sure and slow —
Dying as a dog would die, by the wayside as we go.

"One by one they're falling round us, their pale faces to
the sky;
We've no strength left to dig them graves — there let them
lie.
The wild bird, if he's stricken, is mourned by the others,
But we — we die in Christian land, — we die amid our
brothers,

In the land which God has given, like a wild beast in his
    cave,
Without a tear, a prayer, a shroud, a coffin, or a grave.
Ha! but think ye the contortions on each livid face ye see,
Will not be read on Judgment-day by eyes of Deity?

"We are wretches, famished, scorned, human tools to
    build your pride,
But God will yet take vengeance for the soul for whom
    Christ died.
Now is your hour of pleasure — bask ye in the world's
    caress;
But our whitening bones against ye will rise as witnesses,
From the cabins and the ditches in their charred, un-
    coffined masses,
For the Angel of the Trumpet will know them as he
    passes.
A ghastly spectral army, before great God we'll stand,
And arraign ye as our murderers, O spoilers of our land!"

WILLIAM BUTLER YEATS (1865–1939)

The Cat and the Moon

The cat went here and there
And the moon spun round like a top,
And the nearest kin of the moon,
The creeping cat, looked up.
Black Minnaloushe stared at the moon,
For, wander and wail as he would,
The pure cold light in the sky
Troubled his animal blood.

Minnaloushe runs in the grass
Lifting his delicate feet.
Do you dance, Minnaloushe, do you dance?
When two close kindred meet,
What better than call a dance?
Maybe the moon may learn,
Tired of that courtly fashion,
A new dance turn.
Minnaloushe creeps through the grass
From moonlit place to place,
The sacred moon overhead
Has taken a new phase.
Does Minnaloushe know that his pupils
Will pass from change to change,
And that from round to crescent,
From crescent to round they range?
Minnaloushe creeps through the grass
Alone, important and wise,
And lifts to the changing moon
His changing eyes.

On Being Asked for a War Poem

I think it better that in times like these
A poet's mouth be silent, for in truth
We have no gift to set a statesman right;
He has had enough of meddling who can please
A young girl in the indolence of her youth,
Or an old man upon a winter's night.

To a Child Dancing in the Wind

Dance there upon the shore;
What need have you to care
For wind or water's roar?
And tumble out your hair
That the salt drops have wet;
Being young you have not known
The fool's triumph, nor yet
Love lost as soon as won,
Nor the best labourer dead
And all the sheaves to bind.
What need have you to dread
The monstrous crying of wind?

Politics

*"In our time the destiny of man presents its
meaning in political terms."* — THOMAS MANN

How can I, that girl standing there,
My attention fix
On Roman or on Russian
Or on Spanish politics?
Yet here's a travelled man that knows
What he talks about,
And there's a politician
That has read and thought,
And maybe what they say is true
Of war and war's alarms,
But O that I were young again
And held her in my arms!

Brown Penny

I whispered, "I am too young,"
And then, "I am old enough";
Wherefore I threw a penny
To find out if I might love.
"Go and love, go and love, young man,
If the lady be young and fair."
Ah, penny, brown penny, brown penny,
I am looped in the loops of her hair.
O love is the crooked thing,
There is nobody wise enough
To find out all that is in it,
For he would be thinking of love
Till the stars had run away
And the shadows eaten the moon.
Ah, penny, brown penny, brown penny,
One cannot begin it too soon.

To a Poet, Who Would Have Me Praise Certain Bad Poets, Imitators of His and Mine

You say, as I have often given tongue
In praise of what another's said or sung,
'Twere politic to do the like by these;
But was there ever dog that praised his fleas?

For Anne Gregory

"Never shall a young man,
Thrown into despair
By those great honey-coloured
Ramparts at your ear,
Love you for yourself alone
And not your yellow hair."

"But I can get a hair-dye
And set such colour there,
Brown, or black, or carrot,
That young men in despair
May love me for myself alone
And not my yellow hair."

"I heard an old religious man
But yesternight declare
That he had found a text to prove
That only God, my dear,
Could love you for yourself alone
And not your yellow hair."

All Things Can Tempt Me

All things can tempt me from this craft of verse:
One time it was a woman's face, or worse —
The seeming needs of my fool-driven land;
Now nothing but comes readier to the hand
Than this accustomed toil. When I was young,
I had not given a penny for a song
Did not the poet sing it with such airs
That one believed he had a sword upstairs;
Yet would be now, could I but have my wish,
Colder and dumber and deafer than a fish.

Adam's Curse

We sat together at one summer's end,
That beautiful mild woman, your close friend,
And you and I, and talked of poetry.
I said, "A line will take us hours maybe;
Yet if it does not seem a moment's thought,
Our stitching and unstitching has been naught.

Better go down upon your marrow-bones
And scrub a kitchen pavement, or break stones
Like an old pauper, in all kinds of weather;
For to articulate sweet sounds together
Is to work harder than all these, and yet
Be thought an idler by the noisy set
Of bankers, schoolmasters, and clergymen
The martyrs call the world."

                          And thereupon
That beautiful mild woman for whose sake
There's many a one shall find out all heartache
On finding that her voice is sweet and low
Replied, "To be born woman is to know—
Although they do not talk of it at school—
That we must labour to be beautiful."

I said, "It's certain there is no fine thing
Since Adam's fall but needs much labouring.
There have been lovers who thought love should be
So much compounded of high courtesy
That they would sigh and quote with learned looks
Precedents out of beautiful old books;
Yet now it seems an idle trade enough."

We sat grown quiet at the name of love;
We saw the last embers of daylight die,
And in the trembling blue-green of the sky
A moon, worn as if it had been a shell
Washed by time's waters as they rose and fell
About the stars and broke in days and years.

I had a thought for no one's but your ears:
That you were beautiful, and that I strove
To love you in the old high way of love;
That it had all seemed happy, and yet we'd grown
As weary-hearted as that hollow moon.

He Thinks of Those Who Have Spoken
Evil of His Beloved

Half close your eyelids, loosen your hair,
And dream about the great and their pride;
They have spoken against you everywhere,
But weigh this song with the great and their pride;
I made it out of a mouthful of air,
Their children's children shall say they have lied.

The Lover Tells of the Rose in His Heart

All things uncomely and broken, all things worn out and
old,
The cry of a child by the roadway, the creak of a lumber-
ing cart,
The heavy steps of the ploughman, splashing the wintry
mould,
Are wronging your image that blossoms a rose in the
deeps of my heart.

The wrong of unshapely things is a wrong too great to be
    told;
I hunger to build them anew and sit on a green knoll
    apart,
With the earth and the sky and the water, re-made, like
    a casket of gold
For my dreams of your image that blossoms a rose in the
    deeps of my heart.

The Lamentation of the Old Pensioner

Although I shelter from the rain
Under a broken tree,
My chair was nearest to the fire
In every company
That talked of love or politics,
Ere Time transfigured me.

Though lads are making pikes again
For some conspiracy,
And crazy rascals rage their fill
At human tyranny,
My contemplations are of Time
That has transfigured me.

There's not a woman turns her face
Upon a broken tree,
And yet the beauties that I loved
Are in my memory;
I spit into the face of Time
That has transfigured me.

WILLIAM BUTLER YEATS

The Song of the Old Mother

I rise in the dawn, and I kneel and blow
Till the seed of the fire flicker and glow;
And then I must scrub and bake and sweep
Till stars are beginning to blink and peep;
And the young lie long and dream in their bed
Of the matching of ribbons for bosom and head,
And their day goes over in idleness,
And they sigh if the wind but lift a tress:
While I must work because I am old,
And the seed of the fire gets feeble and cold.

"I Am of Ireland"

"I am of Ireland,
And the Holy Land of Ireland,
And time runs on," cried she.
"Come out of charity,
Come dance with me in Ireland."

One man, one man alone
In that outlandish gear,
One solitary man
Of all that rambled there
Had turned his stately head.
"That is a long way off,
And time runs on," he said,
"And the night grows rough."

"I am of Ireland,
And the Holy Land of Ireland,
And time runs on," cried she.
"Come out of charity
And dance with me in Ireland."

"The fiddlers are all thumbs,
Or the fiddle-string accursed,
The drums and the kettledrums
And the trumpets all are burst,
And the trombone," cried he,
"The trumpet and trombone,"
And cocked a malicious eye,
"But time runs on, runs on."

"I am of Ireland,
And the Holy Land of Ireland,
And time runs on," cried she.
"Come out of charity
And dance with me in Ireland."

BIOGRAPHIES OF THE POETS

WILLIAM ALLINGHAM (1824–1889). Born in Donegal, educated in Ireland, spent most of his life in London as an editor, playwright, and poet. He is best known for his children's poem "The Fairies": "Up the airy mountain,/Down the rushy glen . . . ."

ISAAC BICKERSTAFFE (1735–?1812). Prolific playwright, best known for his "The Miller of Dee," which has become a folk song.

C. J. BOLAND. His grandson Frederick Boland was in recent years the president of the United Nations, and his great-granddaughter is named below.

EAVAN BOLAND (1945–   ). She was an outstanding student at Trinity College, and has been writing and publishing poetry since the age of seventeen. Miss Boland is active as a poetry critic and as a newspaper and radio-TV interviewer on literary matters.

EILEEN BRENNAN (1913–   ). Born in England of Irish parents, educated there and in Ireland, where she now lives.

J. J. CALLANAN (1795–1829). Born in Cork. A teacher most of his life, he was one of the first poets and scholars to make good translations from the Irish.

JOSEPH CAMPBELL (1879–1944). Born in Belfast, spent the nineteen thirties in America as Director of Irish Studies at Fordham University.

ETHNA CARBERY (1866–1902). Born in Belfast, daughter of a Northern Ireland Fenian leader. She was married to the poet and folklorist Seumas MacManus.

EILÉAN NÍ CHUILLEANÁIN (1942–   ). Educated at University College, Cork, and at Oxford. An organizer of poetry readings, she publishes regularly in Irish and English periodicals, and teaches at Trinity College.

AUSTIN CLARKE (1896–   ). Born in County Antrim, educated at University College, Dublin. He has written much verse-drama and helped found a theater for the acting and speaking of verse. A poet, novelist, and playwright, he has also published two volumes of autobiography, and is considered the dean of poets resident in Ireland.

PADRAIC COLUM (1881–   ). Born in Longford. A friend of James Joyce's, he was active in the Irish Literary Renaissance. He has written novels, biographies, plays, and many volumes of poetry. He divides his time between New York and Ireland.

JAMES H. COUSINS (1873–1955). Born in Belfast, helped organize the Irish National Theatre. Late in life, he came to the United States where he taught English at the University of Indiana.

GEORGE DARLEY (1795–1846). Born in Dublin, educated at Trinity College there. He spent most of his life in the London literary world.

THOMAS DAVIS (1814–1845). Born in County Cork, educated at Trinity College, Dublin. He founded the revolutionary newspaper *The Nation,* and helped to establish the Young Ireland party. He wrote all his verse in the last three years of his short life.

C. DAY LEWIS (1904–   ). Born in Northern Ireland, educated at Oxford where he was associated with the group of poets that included W. H. Auden and Stephen Spender. He has written a number of detective novels under the pseudonym of Nicholas Blake. He is presently England's poet laureate.

LORD DUNSANY (1878–1957). Edward John Moreton Drax Plunkett, member of a distinguished Anglo-Irish family from County Meath. Educated in England, he was the author of dozens of books – novels, short stories, plays, and poetry.

FRANCIS A. FAHY (1845–1935). Born in Kinvara, on Galway Bay, spent most of his life in the English Civil Service. He was a prolific writer of Irish songs and ballads.

ROBERT FARREN (1909–   ). Born in Dublin. He taught for several years, and was then put in charge of Irish language broadcasting for Radio Eireann. In 1940 he became a director of the Abbey Theatre. He is the author of a fine book on poetry, *The Course of Irish Verse.*

SIR SAMUEL FERGUSON (1810–1886). Born in Belfast, educated as a lawyer; during a distinguished career in that field became the foremost scholar of Ireland's language and ancient history.

PADRAIC FIACC (1924–   ). Born in Belfast, grew up in New York City. He returned to Ireland in 1947, and is active as a critic and poet. He lives in County Antrim.

ROBIN FLOWER (1881–1946). Born in Yorkshire, England, educated at Oxford University and National University, Dublin. The foremost contemporary scholar on Celtic studies, he lectured on the subject at universities in the United States.

PERCY FRENCH (1854–1922). Born in Roscommon, became famous as a song writer, and toured as a vaudeville singer and entertainer. He is said to have written, and had stolen from him, the song "Abdulla Bulbul Amir."

MONK GIBBON (1896–   ). Son of a clergyman, film and ballet critic, has published a diversity of books — travel, poetry, etc.

OLIVER ST. JOHN GOGARTY (1878–1957). Born in Dublin, in which city he became a successful surgeon. A friend of James Joyce's, he was famed as the wittiest conversationalist in Ireland. He wrote books of literary reminiscences, the best known of which is *As I Was Going Down Sackville Street.*

ALFRED PERCEVAL GRAVES (1846–1931). Born in Dublin, son of the bishop of Limerick. Best known for his adaptations of folk songs from the Irish and the Welsh, he was the father of the poet Robert Graves.

LADY GREGORY (1852–1932). Augusta Gregory, an Anglo-Irish noblewoman, associated with Yeats and the founding of the Abbey Theatre. Irish nationalist, friend of poets and writers, she was also a prolific translator of plays and poetry.

SEAMUS HEANEY (1939–   ). Grew up on a farm in Derry, now lives and teaches in Belfast. He is the most honored and prominent of the younger Irish poets.

JOHN HEWITT (1907–   ). Born in Belfast. He has worked for museums in that city and in Coventry, England, where he now lives.

F. R. HIGGINS (1896–1941). Born in County Mayo, active in the Irish labor movement. He was a friend of Yeats's and managing director of the Abbey Theatre from 1935 until his death.

DOUGLAS HYDE (1860–1946). Born in Roscommon, educated at Trinity College, Dublin. Active in the Irish nationalist movement, he was president of the Irish Free State (1938–1941). A famous Gaelic scholar, he is generally credited with keeping the Irish language alive through his work with the Gaelic League.

VALENTIN IREMONGER (1918–   ). A member of the Irish Foreign Service, now stationed in New Delhi, India. He has published two anthologies of Irish writing as well as volumes of his own poetry.

PATRICK KAVANAGH (1905–1967). Grew up on a farm in County Monaghan. His best-known poem is the long "The Great Hunger." A controversial figure on the Dublin literary scene for many years, he wrote novels and edited a newspaper.

PEADAR KEARNEY (1883–1942). Born in Dublin, active in the Irish Republican Army. He wrote the lyrics of the Irish national anthem, "The Soldier's Song," and was the uncle of Brendan Behan.

RICHARD KELL (1927–   ). Born in Cork, educated in India, in Belfast, and at Trinity College, Dublin. He now lives in England.

BRENDAN KENNELLY (1936–   ). Born in County Kerry, educated at Trinity College, Dublin. Active on the Irish literary scene, he has lectured in the United States and published seven volumes of poetry and two novels.

CHARLES J. KICKHAM (1830–1882). Born in Tipperary, an ardent Irish patriot. He wrote the well-known novel *Knocknagow.*

THOMAS KINSELLA (1928–   ). Born in Dublin, worked with

Ireland's Department of Finance until 1965. A prolific and distinguished poet and translator, he now teaches, at times, in the United States.

FRANCIS LEDWIDGE (1891–1917). Born in County Meath, a country boy who was befriended and encouraged in his poetry by Lord Dunsany. He was killed in France in the First World War.

SHANE LESLIE (1885–1971). Born in London, son of an Irish baronet, cousin of Winston Churchill. He was educated at Eton and Cambridge, and is the author of many novels and biographies.

WINIFRID M. LETTS (1882–   ). As well as poetry, she has written children's books and had two plays produced at the Abbey Theatre.

CHARLES LEVER (1806–1872). Had a long and distinguished career as a physician. He wrote many novels, and almost all his poetry first appeared as parts of his novels.

SAMUEL LOVER (1797–1868). He was for forty-seven years a successful painter. When his eyesight began to fail, he turned to song writing, and performed publicly. His most famous book is the novel *Handy Andy*.

DONAGH MACDONAGH (1912–1968). Born in Dublin, educated at University College, the son of the poet Thomas MacDonagh. He also wrote plays, the best known of which is *Happy as Larry*.

THOMAS MACDONAGH (1878–1916). Born in Tipperary, studied for the priesthood, but instead became a teacher and a Gaelic scholar. He was executed by the English for his part in the Easter Week Rebellion.

PATRICK MACDONOGH (1902–1961). Educated at Trinity College, Dublin. A teacher and a commercial artist, and eventually an executive in a brewery, he published four volumes of verse.

MÁIRE MACENTEE (1922–   ). Worked for many years in the Irish diplomatic service, where she met and married the author and statesman Conor Cruise O'Brien. She is noted as an Irish scholar.

SEUMAS MACMANUS (1869–1960). Born in Donegal, was a schoolteacher and a collector of Irish folk tales. He became a well-known *shanachie* (teller of legends) and as such made many tours of the United States.

LOUIS MACNEICE (1907–1963). Born in Belfast, educated at Oxford University. A teacher and a writer for the British Broadcasting Corporation, he was also the author of many books, some of them written in collaboration with W. H. Auden.

DEREK MAHON (1941–   ). Born in Belfast, educated at Trinity College, Dublin. He spent two years in Canada and the United States, and now teaches in Ireland.

JAMES CLARENCE MANGAN (1803–1849). Born in Dublin. He had no formal education, but began working at fifteen. Always poor and in ill health, he had a flair for languages and passed off many of his original poems as translations.

KUNO MEYER (1859–1919). Born in Germany, became one of the greatest Celtic scholars and translators, teaching at Liverpool University and in Berlin. He was also co-founder and director of the Summer School of Irish Learning in Dublin.

ALICE MILLIGAN (1880–1953). Born in County Tyrone, educated in Belfast and London. With Ethna Carbery, she founded and edited a nationalist literary paper, *The Shan Van Vocht.*

JOHN MONTAGUE (1929–   ). Born in Brooklyn, N.Y., of Irish parents, went to Ireland at four, and grew up on an Ulster farm. He was educated at University College, Dublin, and Yale University. He now lives most of the year in Paris with his French wife.

THOMAS MOORE (1779–1852). Born in Dublin, the son of a grocer, and educated at Trinity College there. He became a popular figure in English society, where he performed, singing the lyrics he set to old Irish airs. A friend of Lord Byron and all the other literary elite of the time, he was the first Irish-Catholic poet to gain an international reputation.

RICHARD MURPHY (1927–   ). Born in Galway, spent most of his early years in Ceylon. Educated in England, he now lives on the west coast of Ireland, where he operates a large sea-fishing boat.

T. D. O'BOLGER (19?–   ). Born in Ireland. For many years he has lived in the United States, where he taught at the University of Pennsylvania.

FRANK O'CONNOR (1903–1966). Born in Cork as Michael O'Donovan; became a librarian, then an associate of AE and Yeats with the Abbey Theatre. Ireland's best-known short-story writer, he was also a noted scholar and translator. During the fifties he lived in the United States and taught at Harvard and Stanford, among other places.

SEÁN O'CRÍADÁIN (1930–   ). Born in Cork. Lived in London and Rome, where he edited the literary magazine *Botteghe Oscure*. He divides his time between New York and Dublin, and was recently one of the poets included in the book *Five Irish Poets*.

EUGENE O'CURRY (1796–1862). Born in County Clare. Professor of Irish History and Archaeology at the Catholic University in Dublin, he is noted as a preserver and restorer of ancient Irish manuscripts.

SEAN O'FAOLAIN (1900–   ). Novelist, short-story writer, biographer, playwright, and teacher. He has also written biographies of Daniel O'Connell and Eamon De Valera. His best-known novel is *A Nest of Simple Folk*.

DESMOND O'GRADY (1935–   ). Born in Limerick. He has lived in Paris and Rome, where he now teaches at a boys' school.

MOIRA O'NEILL (1863–1955). Born in County Antrim, lived for some years in the Canadian Rockies. Her best-known book is *Songs from the Glens of Antrim*.

ARTHUR O'SHAUGHNESSY (1844–1881). Born in either Dublin or London. He worked for the British Museum all his life; he was a friend of contemporary French poets.

D. J. O'SULLIVAN (1906–   ). Born in County Cork. His family has a tradition of being lighthouse keepers, and he is one, stationed off the Donegal coast. He is a well-known naturalist.

SEUMAS O'SULLIVAN (1879–1958). Pseudonym of James Sullivan Starkey. He was for many years the influential editor of the *Dublin Magazine;* he published seven volumes of verse.

BASIL PAYNE (1928–   ). Lives in Dublin, where he is employed by the Irish government; has translated work of young German poets.

PADRAIC PEARSE (1879–1916). Born in Dublin, where he founded St. Enda's School. He was active in the fight for Irish freedom; his funeral oration at the grave of the Fenian leader, O'Donovan Rossa, is credited with stirring up the patriotic feeling which led to the Easter Rebellion of 1916. He was executed by the English.

JOSEPH MARY PLUNKETT (1887–1916). Born in Dublin, active in the Irish theater. An editor of the *Irish Review,* he was executed by the English for his share in the Easter Rebellion.

FATHER PROUT (1804–1866). Pseudonym of Francis Sylvester Mahony. Born in Cork, he became a priest but left the order under a special dispensation. A prolific literary man, he contributed "The Father Prout Papers" to *Fraser's* magazine. He traveled extensively, and died in Paris. Mahony said of Father Prout, "His brain was a storehouse in inexhaustible knowledge, and his memory a bazaar."

W. R. RODGERS (1909–1969). Born in Belfast. A Presbyterian minister in County Armagh, he subsequently became a scriptwriter and producer for the British Broadcasting Corporation.

THOMAS WILLIAM ROLLESTON (1857–1920). Born in King's County, educated at Trinity College, Dublin. He was an expert translator from German, Greek, and Irish.

GEORGE WILLIAM RUSSELL (1867–1935). Used the pseudonym AE. Born in County Armagh; a poet, a mystic, and a painter; a focal point for literary Dublin during the Irish Literary Renaissance; friend of Yeats, Stephens, Patrick Kavanagh.

RICHARD RYAN (1946–   ). Young Dublin poet and college student, editor of a poetry broadsheet. His first book of verse was published in 1970.

JAMES STEPHENS (1881–1950). Born in Dublin. He never had a formal education but became a typist in a law office. His writing attracted the attention of George William Russell (AE), who introduced him to the Dublin literary world. His most famous book is *The Crock of Gold.*

L. A. G. STRONG (1896–1958). Born in England, spent his formative years in Dublin. He was a prolific novelist. Many of his novels are set in Ireland, as is his collection of verse, *Dublin Poems*.

JONATHAN SWIFT (1667–1745). Born in Dublin. The most famous satirist in the English language, author of *Gulliver's Travels*, he was the dean of St. Patrick's Cathedral in Dublin from 1713 until his death.

JOHN MILLINGTON SYNGE (1871–1909). Born near Dublin, graduated from Trinity College. He was a friend of Yeats's and a great playwright whose most famous works—*Riders to the Sea* and *Playboy of the Western World*—were written during the last five years of his short life.

JOHN TODHUNTER (1839–1916). Born in Dublin of Quaker parents, graduated from Trinity College there. Physician, teacher, and playwright, he was one of the founders of the Irish Literary Society in London, where he lived the major part of his life.

HERBERT TRENCH (1865–1923). Educated at Oxford, director of London's Haymarket Theatre, resident much of his life in Italy.

JOHN FRANCIS WALLER (1810–1894). Graduate of Trinity College, Dublin, member of the Irish Bar, he wrote five books of verse.

JOAN WATTON (1942–   ). A young poet from Northern Ireland.

RICHARD WEBER (1932–   ). Born in Dublin. One of the most widely published of the younger Irish poets, he has spent some years living in London and Italy.

LADY WILDE (1826–1896). Wife of a noted Dublin physician and mother of Oscar Wilde, she wrote under the pen name "Speranza."

WILLIAM BUTLER YEATS (1865–1939). Born near Dublin. The most celebrated and influential poet of his century, he was also a playwright, a critic, and founder of the Abbey Theatre.

ACKNOWLEDGMENTS

The compiler of *Poems from Ireland* and the Thomas Y. Crowell Company wish to thank the following authors, editors, publishers, and agents for granting permission to reprint copyrighted material. All possible care has been taken to trace ownership of every selection included and to make full acknowledgment for its use. If any errors have accidentally occurred, they will be corrected in subsequent editions, provided notification is sent to the publisher.

Barrie & Jenkins Ltd. for "The Wife of Llew" and "Had I a Golden Pound" by Francis Ledwidge, from *Complete Poems.*

Ernest Benn Limited for "Muckish Mountain" and "Prayer for Fine Weather" by Shane Leslie, from *Poems and Ballads.*

Simon Campbell for "Three Colts Exercising in a Six-Acre," "Butterfly in the Fields," and "Blanaid's Song" by Joseph Campbell, from *Poems from Ireland (The Irish Times).*

Jonathan Cape Ltd., The Hogarth Press, and Harold Matson Company, Inc. for "Jig" by C. Day Lewis, from *Collected Poems,* copyright 1954 by C. D. Lewis.

Chatto and Windus Ltd. for "Citadels" by Richard Kell, from *Control Tower.*

Eiléan Ní Chuilleanáin for "Swine Herd" published in *The Irish Times,* copyright Eiléan Ní Chuilleanáin 1970.

The Clarendon Press for "Pangur Bán" from *The Irish Tradition* and "The Passage at Night," from *The Western Island,* translated by Robin Flower.

The Devin-Adair Company for "To a Late Poplar," "Inniskeen Road: July Evening," and "Pegasus" by Patrick Kavanagh, from *Collected Poems,* copyright 1964 by Patrick Kavanagh; "O Boys!" and "Back from the Country" by Oliver St. John Gogarty, from *Collected Poems,* copyright 1954 by Oliver St. John Gogarty; "River-Mates," "The Poor Girl's Meditation," "Interior," and "A Drover" by Padraic Colum, from *Collected Poems,* copyright 1953 by Padraic Colum; "I Tell Her She Is Lovely" by Monk Gibbon, "The Boy and the Geese" and "Deranged" by Padraic Fiacc, "One Kingfisher and One Yellow Rose" by Eileen Brennan, "The Widow of Drynam," "Dodona's Oaks Were Still," "Song," and "She Walked Unaware" by Patrick MacDonogh, and "Drinking Time" by D. J. O'Sullivan, all from *New Irish Poets,* copyright © 1947 by Devin-Adair Company.

The Dolmen Press Limited for "For the Moment" and "Stephen's Green Revisited" by Richard Weber, from *Stephen's Green Revisited;* "The Thrush's Nest" by Richard Ryan, from *Ledges;* "Irish Curse on the Occupying English" by Máire MacEntee from *A Heart Full of Thought;* "The Planter's Daughter" and "Irish-American Dignitary" by Austin Clarke, from *Later Poems;* "A Strong Wind" by Austin Clarke, from *Flight to Africa;* "Thirty-three Triads" by Thomas Kinsella, from *Poems and Translations.*

Edward Plunkett, Lord Dunsany, for "A Call to the Wild."

Faber & Faber for "Droit de Seigneur" by Richard Murphy, from *Sailing to an Island;* "Dublin Made Me" and "A Revel" by Donagh MacDonagh, from *The Hungry Grass;* "Prayer Before Birth," "Glass Falling," and "Dublin" by Louis MacNeice, from *The Collected Poems of Louis MacNeice,* copyright © by The Estate of Louis MacNeice 1966; "Follower" by Seamus Heaney, from *Death of a Naturalist,* © 1966 by Seamus Heaney; "The Forge" by Seamus Heaney, from *Door into the Dark,* © 1969 by Seamus Heaney.

Farrar, Straus & Giroux, Inc. for "Armagh" by W. R. Rodgers, from *Europa and the Bull,* copyright 1952 by W. R. Rodgers.

Allen Figgis & Co. Ltd. for "The Black Cliffs, Ballybunion" by Brendan Kennelly, from *Dream of a Black Fox;* "Light Dying" by Brendan Kennelly, from *Collection One;* "Requiem for a Personal Friend" by Eavan Boland, from *A New Territory,* copyright Allen Figgis & Co. Ltd. 1967.

Victor Gollancz Ltd. for "The Discovery" by Monk Gibbon, from *For Daws to Peck At,* copyright 1929 by Monk Gibbon.

William Heinemann Ltd. for "Requiem of a War-Baby" by Joan Watton, from *Young Commonwealth Poets,* edited by P. L. Brent, published by William Heinemann Ltd. in association with Cardiff Commonwealth Arts Festival.

John Hewitt for "In This Year of Grace" (*The Irish Times*), © John Hewitt 1969; "O Country People," from *Collected Poems 1934–67* (MacGibbon & Kee Ltd.), © John Hewitt 1968.

May Higgins for "At Flock Mass," "Father and Son," and "Padraic O'Conaire, Gaelic Storyteller."

Valentin Iremonger for "This Houre Her Vigill" and "Spring Stops Me Suddenly" by Valentin Iremonger, from *Poems from Ireland* (*The Irish Times*).

Richard Kell for "The Makers."

Alfred A. Knopf, Inc. for "A Man of Experience," "Kilcash," and "The Harper," from *Kings, Lords, and Commons* by Frank O'Connor, copyright © 1959 by Frank O'Connor.

ACKNOWLEDGMENTS

The Macmillan Company, The Macmillan Company of Canada Limited, Macmillan London and Basingstoke, and Mrs. Iris Wise for "To the Four Courts, Please," "Nora Criona," "Bessie Bobtail," "The Wind," "The Devil's Bag," "The County Mayo," and "The Centaurs" by James Stephens, from *Collected Poems;* "I Am Raftery" by James Stephens, from *Reincarnations;* copyright 1909, 1912, 1915, 1918 by The Macmillan Company, copyright renewed 1940, 1943, 1946 by James Stephens.

The Macmillan Company, The Macmillan Company of Canada Limited, and Michael B. Yeats for "Adam's Curse," "He Thinks of Those Who Have Spoken Evil of His Beloved," "The Song of the Old Mother," "The Lover Tells of the Rose in His Heart," "The Lamentation of the Old Pensioner," "Brown Penny," "To a Poet, Who Would Have Me Praise Certain Bad Poets, Imitators of His and Mine," "All Things Can Tempt Me," "To a Child Dancing in the Wind," "The Cat and the Moon," "On Being Asked for a War Poem," "For Anne Gregory," "I Am of Ireland," and "Politics" by William Butler Yeats, from *Collected Poems,* copyright 1903, 1906, 1912, 1916, 1919, 1933 by The Macmillan Company, 1940 by Georgie Yeats, copyright renewed 1931, 1934 by William Butler Yeats, 1940, 1944, 1947, 1961 by Bertha Georgie Yeats, 1968 by Bertha Georgie Yeats, Michael Butler Yeats and Anne Yeats.

Seán O'Críadáin for "Great-Aunts," copyright © 1970 by Seán O'Críadáin.

Harriet R. O'Donovan for "Three Old Brothers" by Frank O'Connor, from *Centaur Poets.*

Oxford University Press, Inc. (New York) for "Prayer Before Birth," "Glass Falling," and "Dublin" by Louis MacNeice, from *The Collected Poems of Louis MacNeice,* edited by E. R. Dodds, copyright © by The Estate of Louis MacNeice 1966; "Follower" by Seamus Heaney, from *Death of a Naturalist,* © 1966 by Seamus Heaney; "The Forge" by Seamus Heaney, from *Door into the Dark,* © 1969 by Seamus Heaney.

Oxford University Press (London) for "Is It a Month" by John Millington Synge, from *Collected Works of J. M. Synge,* edited by Robin Skelton ("In Glencullen," "A Question" and "Patch-Shaneen" also from Oxford edition); "The Prisoner" and "Exit Molloy" by Derek Mahon, from *Night Crossing.* Basil Payne for "Angry Old Men," from *Sunlight on a Square* (John Augustine & Co., Dublin, 1961).

A. D. Peters & Company for "Murphy in Manchester" by John Montague, from *Poisoned Lands;* "The Trout" and "Time Out" by John Montague, from *A Chosen Light;* "A Memory," "The Mad-Woman," and "The Knowledgeable Child" by L. A. G. Strong, from *Selected Poems.*

Russell & Volkening for "The Vesture of the Soul" by George William Russell.

ACKNOWLEDGMENTS

Martin Secker & Warburg Ltd. for "White Christmas" and "The Fountains" by W. R. Rodgers, from *Awake and Other Poems'* "Armagh" by W. R. Rodgers, from *Europa and the Bull.*

Sheed & Ward, Inc. for "Rich Morning" by Robert Farren, from *Selected Poems.*

Dr. Michael Solomons, executor, for "A Blessing on the Cows," "Cottage," "A Piper," "The Convent," and "Rain" by Seumas O'Sullivan, from *Dublin Poems,* copyright 1940 by the Executor of the late Mrs. E. F. Starkey.

The Swallow Press, Inc., Chicago, for "Afternoon" by Desmond O'Grady, from *New Poets of Ireland,* © 1963.

The Viking Press, Inc. for "Summer Is Gone" by Sean O'Faolain, from *The Silver Branch,* copyright 1938, copyright © renewed 1966 by Sean O'Faolain.

INDEX OF POETS

INDEX OF TITLES

INDEX OF FIRST LINES